BEING TED WILLIAMS

Growing Up with a Baseball Idol

DICK ENBERG
with Tom Clavin

SPORTS
PUBLISHING

Sports Publishing books may be purchased in bulk at special discounts for sales promotion, corporate gifts, fund-raising, or educational purposes. Special editions can also be created to specifications. For details, contact the Special Sales Department, Sports Publishing, 307 West 36th Street, 11th Floor, New York, NY 10018 or sportspubbooks@ skyhorsepublishing.com.

Sports Publishing® is a registered trademark of Skyhorse Publishing, Inc.®, a Delaware corporation.

Visit our website at www.sportspubbooks.com.

10 9 8 7 6 5 4 3 2 1

Library of Congress Cataloging-in-Publication Data is available on file.

Cover design by Brian Peterson
Cover photo courtesy of Dick Enberg

ISBN: 978-1-68358-221-2
Ebook ISBN: 978-1-68358-222-9

Printed in the United States of America

Contents

Author's Note

The basic motivation for writing this book was to relate the extraordinary path taken while following my baseball idol, Ted Williams—also known as the Splendid Splinter, Teddy Ballgame, and Thumper, but mostly as the Kid. Thanks to being influenced by my grandfather (he loved Charlie Gehringer and Tommy Bridges), who claimed to have attended 35 consecutive Detroit Tigers season openers, and by his daughter, my mother, who teethed me on a miniature baseball bat, and a father who fluttered his fork ball as a teenage pitcher in Northern Minnesota's Iron Ore Range, I have special DNA, the kind infused by baseball.

From my kindergarten years, my dream was to be a baseball player. At family reunions, I received the usual prerequisite queries from relatives, "Dickie, what are you going to be when you grow up?" No hesitation from me. Confidently, I'd answer, "I'm going to be a ballplayer."

One of my earliest memories is at age 4 in my grandfather's small corner neighborhood grocery store in Mt. Clemens, Michigan. He'd coach me on some simple baseball trivia and ask me later to repeat each baseball fact. If correct, he'd reach up on the candy shelf and reward me with some "Superman Bubble Gum." Perhaps in a subtle way he was preparing me for my desire to be like my personal super-hero, Ted Williams, a human baseball vessel in which I could pour my hopes and dreams.

Over time, Theodore Samuel Williams would become much more than my hero. He would eventually become a friend. My dreams took me to a great place. And that has continued through the process of writing this book. I have learned of qualities of my idol that have forti-fied my pride in trying to be like him. Not just his enormous talent, as arguably the greatest hitter in the last eight decades of modern base-ball, but his off-the-field generosity and sense of fairness to his fellow man. He cared about the little guy, the sick and injured, and the inclu-sion of black players in baseball. Superhero stuff.

Another advantage to having sports heroes in our youth is that many of us spend lifetimes arguing with others as to which heroes were the best. As time passes, our idols don't disappear, but rather they remain part of us. We build on their extraordinary exploits, and it's certainly fair game to magnify their heroic feats. For baseball fans, it is both a comfort and a thrill to rock away on the front porch reminiscing about the amazing achievements of Ted Williams, Willie Mays, Mickey Mantle, Roberto Clemente, Jackie Robinson, Henry Aaron, and others who are permanent residents of Cooperstown.

More than a few readers of *Being Ted Williams* will contend that "the Kid" had a dark side. Indeed, he did. He stumbled and failed as a husband and father. He would make an old sailor blush with his wild profanity. He abhorred baseball writers. Sufficiently provoked by boo-birds, Ted would rather spit at fans than tip his cap to them. Duly noted, and there is no sugarcoating it. But this book is *not* about that side of the man. We don't strip the veneer of our comic and movie superheroes in order to discover what's wrong. They give us cause to celebrate what they do right, or at least better than most others. We stand to cheer their spectacular victories against the bad guys, each effort building on the next. It's interesting that Superman has survived my entire life, as have Wonder Woman and Batman. They live on because we support and celebrate their courage, their physical and mental brilliance, their fiercely driven battle for good against evil. There's no reason to search for any personal faults. Hey, they're *superheroes*, that's what they do.

My Superman was Ted Williams . . . even if there was some pine tar on his cape. This book tells you why, and about his career and what very few people saw and knew about him. Being Ted Williams was never easy . . . but idolizing him was.

This is not necessarily a biography of Ted Williams, but I was helped enormously by a couple of terrific biographies and a few other books that provided a wealth of information and insight. I want to especially acknowledge *Ted Williams: The Biography of An American Hero* by Leigh Montville, *The Kid: The Immortal Life of Ted Williams* by Ben Bradlee Jr., and two books by David Halberstam, *Summer of '49* and *The Teammates*. Also helpful was *My Turn at Bat*, Ted's autobiography, written with John Underwood. (Except where noted, all quotes by Ted are from this book.) I'm sure the autobiography revealed a lot more about Ted's career and especially his life than he ever intended.

One last note: My thanks to George Mitrovich, my friend and fellow baseball lover, who introduced me to Tom Clavin and, like it or not, bears some responsibility for this book.

Prologue: Summer 1946

Preadolescence is fraught with fantasies and fears. Dreaming can be a kid's panacea in such immature times. Dreaming is finding hope, happiness, and even make-believe heroism in some undefined but safe place. It is there to find idols, bigger in life because we have made them so. They flourish in our full imagination. Mine did.

For me, it began in July 1946. There was no more World War II-imposed gas rationing. The Enbergs of the San Fernando Valley in California along with all Americans could exercise all the fun and freedom of unrestricted travel. We were making a first-ever visit to San Francisco to visit my father's best friend, a fellow Finn from his schoolboy days. They grew in Northern Minnesota's iron ore country, the Mesabi Range.

While the men "yo-yo-yoed" (that's what Finns do when humored) over a cold beer, the women shared baby talk in the kitchen. My sister, Sharyl, was not yet a year old. I was left happily alone and was sitting mesmerized in front of the large console living-room radio. The vivid descriptions provided by the play-by-play announcers, Mel Allen and Jim Britt, of the 1946 Baseball All-Star Game guided my imagination. I had already decided, announcing to all who would hear, that when I grew up I was going to be a ballplayer. Perhaps that was a factor in my "seeing" that radio report in such full color—it was captivating.

There was an especially exciting feel to the Summer Classic that year because it was being held at Fenway Park in Boston, and the Red Sox were on the way to their first American League pennant since 1918. They had eight players on the American League All-Star team—Boo Ferriss, Hal Wagner, Mickey Harris, Rudy York, Johnny Pesky, Bobby Doerr, and in the outfield, Dominic DiMaggio and Ted Williams.

In the bottom of the eighth inning, Truett "Rip" Sewell of the Pittsburgh Pirates was on the mound and Williams was at the plate. The string bean outfielder, just back from his three years of military service, had already hit one home run and two singles in the game. I and millions of other listeners were told that Sewell smiled at Williams, who responded by shaking his head. Everyone knew what would come next: Sewell was going to throw his "eephus" pitch, a slow overhand toss that traveled in a 20-foot arc before dropping into the catcher's mitt. Normally, batters were so unfamiliar with its tantalizing trajectory that few could time it properly, and if they did, they had to supply all the power.

Sewell, proudly, had never given up a home run on his eephus pitch. But being in the National League, Sewell had not faced Ted Williams before. By shaking his head, Williams was trying to talk him out of it . . . to no avail.

Sewell nodded. This was the moment. He went into his full windup as though about to whip a fastball down the middle, but out of his right hand came the blooper. Williams's eyes expanded to fried eggs, and he swung from his heels. Foul ball. Sewell nodded again, the same pitch, but it was outside, ball one. Then he snuck a fastball in for a strike, 1-2 count. The capacity crowd was all keyed up. So was Williams. Then came the next eephus in its slow, tantalizing arc.

Williams couldn't contain himself. Not waiting for the ball to even enter the batter's box, he hopped forward twice and swung. He connected, and now the ball had a different arc . . . one that took it high and far into the summer-afternoon sky, to land in the A.L. bullpen. Williams laughed as he trotted around the bases, and Sewell joined in.

Back in San Francisco, I could only imagine the ball's majestic path. (In fact, this was a time when the daily sports pages would define such moments with a long-distance photo using a dotted line to trace the path of the home run ball. In this case, it was from Williams in the batter's box to the eventual landing spot of the home run.) To the kid squatting, listening in front of the radio, with one swing Ted Williams had molded fantasy and the fantastic into reality. I wanted to be like him, a baseball superman. I'd even teach myself to bat left-handed. Maybe that would help. I wanted to be Ted Williams. I was eleven years old. My boyhood dreams would lead to a lifetime inspiration. Trying to be Ted Williams took me on a wondrous ride.

After that baseball season, my family would move from Southern California to Michigan to live on a 40-acre fruit farm, which grew mostly apples and was purchased by my father on the visit preceding our stop in San Francisco. Little did I know that the move to a little village north of Detroit would take me closer to the man the scribes tagged as the "Splendid Splinter." We didn't have any luxuries on the farm, no indoor plumbing and a well that went dry every summer, but we did have an abundance of farmland rocks, many perfectly sized, ideal to simulate baseballs.

I created my own game, while attending our roadside fruit stand, hitting rocks with an old bat. Basic rules: hit it from the farm side over the paved road for a single, doubles cleared the far side culvert, and home runs flew past the telephone wire that hung over the distant field. I would bat right-handed for those who hit from that side and left-handed for Williams and others who swung lefty. And I was calling the shots in my make-believe lineups. (Maybe this is where I first learned to call a good game.)

As I was hitting rocks in 1947, my idol was rocking American League pitchers, hitting .343 with 32 homers and 114 RBIs, capturing the AL Triple Crown, yet losing the American League MVP Award by one point (202-201) to Joe DiMaggio. One writer didn't include

Williams in the top 10 on his ballot, literally stealing the honor from Ted. When the announcement came, I cried. Yet this total injustice only furthered my adoration. At age 12, I knew right from wrong. The good guys still win in my dreams.

And it wouldn't be long before I'd be "that close," witnessing first-hand the greatest hitter I'd ever see . . . and, eventually, becoming his friend.

Part I
The Kid

Ted Williams was that rare 20th-century San Diego citizen—he was born and raised there. I have called the city home for over 20 years, and during that time I have met hundreds of residents who hailed from New York, Boston, Florida, Texas, Colorado, and everywhere in between. Military personnel, especially Navy and Marines who were stationed at nearby bases, often return to begin new careers or retire in San Diego. And, of course, the city became an oasis for those who could not tolerate one more winter back east.

But Ted was born in a different San Diego and century—a hundred years ago, in 1918. As he wrote in his 1969 autobiography, *My Turn at Bat*, "I lived in a small town, which San Diego was then, and in a small town you're not as insulated. You get to know people, you know your neighbors." This turned out to be a big benefit to Ted, who would find his neighbors more caring than his family when it came to his well-being.

The second of eight children, Ted's mother had been born to Pablo and Natalia Venzor in 1891. The family lived in Chihuahua, Mexico. To escape civil unrest, in 1907, when May Venzor was 16, the entire family of eight crossed the border into California and settled in Santa

Barbara, where Pablo worked as a stonemason and a sheep herder. During his youth and playing career, Ted would hide the fact that he was half-Mexican. As he finally admitted in his autobiography, "If I had my mother's name, there is no doubt I would have run into problems in those days, the prejudices people had in Southern California."

The same could have been said about Major League Baseball in the 1930s and '40s. And his own heritage, kept secret for decades, could be why throughout his life Ted was sensitive to any bias in baseball and openly fought prejudices directed at nonwhite players.

May's calling was not necessarily to be a mother, but to be a soldier in the Salvation Army. As a young woman, she became one of its most ardent fundraisers and recruiters as well as a contributor to efforts to convert alcoholics, drug addicts, prostitutes, and others on the edge of society to Christianity. Her territory extended from Los Angeles to San Diego, and sometimes her missions took her across the border to Mexico, inspiring her nickname the "Angel of Tijuana." By the time she met her future husband, she was a lieutenant in the Salvation Army.

Samuel Stuart Williams was born in Ardsley, New York, in 1886. He joined the US Army in 1904 (falsely contending, years later, that he had been one of Teddy Roosevelt's Rough Riders in Cuba in 1898), and he was discharged honorably seven years later. While stationed in Hawaii, he had met a visitor to the island, May Venzor. In his 1969 memoir, Ted would describe her as "not a big woman. She was short and lithe, with one of those infectious Eisenhower smiles." May was reduced in rank from lieutenant to "envoy status," just above a beginner, as a result of marrying someone who was not a Salvation Army member.

She and Sam moved to San Diego in 1915, when it had a population of only 55,000. Three years later, after two stillborn children, May gave birth on August 30 at the Sunshine Maternity Home. The boy was listed as Teddy Samuel Williams, named after Sam's supposed commander, Teddy Roosevelt. (Later, the first name would be changed to Theodore, and further down the road Ted would legally drop Samuel.) The big event in the city in 1915 was the Panama Canal Exposition, held to celebrate the canal's completion. Sam Williams eked out a living operating a photography studio, and as soon as she was up and able, May went back to work for the Salvation Army. In 1920, Daniel Arthur Williams was born, and again May couldn't return to her evangelical duties on the streets fast enough.

Many years later, Ted told me that San Diego allowed young men to blossom there. He certainly did . . . but what determined the development of his personal character, his dynamic temperament, his anger, and his intense resolution to succeed?

Ted and his brother, Danny, spent much of their early years fending for themselves, either together or apart, thanks to their parents' disinterest and their own separate interests. May was a tireless foot soldier, and it seemed that only reluctantly did she return to her "other" family. In his prize-winning biography, *The Kid: The Immortal Life of Ted Williams*, Ben Bradlee Jr. quotes from a newspaper editorial in the 1920s, "to thousands of San Diegans, rich and poor, Mrs. Williams IS the Salvation Army."

In his autobiography, Ted recalled in his usual blunt way that his mom was gone most hours of the day, working at the Salvation Army, and his dad wasn't around much, either. He acknowledges that there were housekeepers who came and went.

Neighbors reported seeing the two young boys sitting together on the front steps until late at night, watching for at least one parent to come home. Worse, though, for the boys was when their mother dragged them to attend Salvation Army street-corner revival meetings.

With increasing frequency, Sam didn't come home. Eventually, he would leave altogether and live apart from his family. Surely this was a big reason why Ted took passionately to sports, especially baseball. His mother's brother Saul was a sandlot pitcher in Santa Barbara (family lore claims he had struck out Babe Ruth during a 1935 barnstorming tour). Whenever May brought her children north to visit her family, or they motored to San Diego, Saul taught Ted how to play.

Back in San Diego, the boy's passion for baseball grew exponentially. He played before school, at lunchtime, and after school until it was too dark to see. Looking back years later, Ted admitted he didn't know how it was possible for anyone to have such a strong desire to play as he did.

***

As a young kid, I was even more ambitious than Ted Williams. He just wanted to be the best hitter in baseball. I wanted to be a great athlete. One of us, at least, fulfilled his dream.

Ted was a 16-year-old high school ballplayer when I was born in January 1935 in Mount Clemens, Michigan. We lived in that small town north of Detroit for just two years, moving first to Bridgeport, Connecticut, and then in 1940, with my one-year-old brother, Dennis, in tow, to Los Angeles. We settled in the rural San Fernando Valley, one hundred miles north of San Diego, which featured dirt roads, small farms, and orange and walnut groves. It was a great place for a kid drawn to sports because essentially it was summer all year long.

I didn't feel deprived that there was no major league baseball team because we had the Los Angeles Angels and the Hollywood Stars in the Pacific Coast League. Some weeks when I emerged from Sunday School, my dad, whose parents had emigrated from Finland, was waiting to take me to doubleheaders at either Wrigley Field or Gilmore Stadium, where I'd feel like I was in heaven. I wished those games would never end, but when they did, many times when we got home, my dad and I would gather our mitts and take turns as pitcher and catcher. The rest of the week, I'd follow the Angels and Stars by listening to Fred Haney announcing their home games on the radio. Later, Haney would go from the broadcast booth to the diamond when he embarked on a career as a manager. He was pretty successful at it, with his Milwaukee Braves beating the New York Yankees in the 1957 World Series, and when Gene Autry acquired the American

League rights for the expansion Los Angeles Angels, Haney became the club's first general manager.

Obviously, he was an influence because when I created games between those two teams on the vacant half-acre lot next to my house, I announced the action. With a bat and tennis ball I imitated every player, hitting lefty and righty. It never occurred to me then that my way into sports was through a broadcast booth, not a baseball diamond. I ate and slept baseball, and my parents never tried to discourage me.

Though I wasn't born there, I couldn't imagine living anywhere else but Southern California. This was one of the few times my imagination let me down.

***

Ted also had no childhood hobbies or interests beyond baseball. That was it and everything. Only having to attend school prevented him from playing from the time he awakened until he reluctantly went to sleep. The Williams family's small house on Utah Street was just a block and a half from the diamond in the North Park playground, and that became his home away from home. During his junior high years, he played for the school team, the local American Legion team, sandlot teams, and any games he and a few friends could scare up.

He had his own baseball heroes. There was a photo of Babe Ruth on his bedroom wall, but if there was any player he considered imitating, it was Bill Terry, who played for the New York Giants. Ironically, if not for Ted's .406 batting average in 1941, Terry would still be the last major league player to bat over .400, which he accomplished in 1930. Another hero was Pepper Martin of the St. Louis Cardinals, the most "western" team in Major League Baseball.

Ted played baseball from 10th through 12th grade at Hoover High, pitching as well as playing the outfield. And boy, could he pitch. Williams held the San Diego section single-game strikeout record, 19 against Redondo High School, for decades. During his very first practice, Ted angered the school janitor by hitting a couple of balls onto the roof of the cafeteria. However, hitting prodigious homers delighted his coach, Wos Caldwell, and Ted continued to do so for the next three years. He finished his high school career with a total .430 average, including an incredible .538 in his junior year.

Nick Canepa, the "Sports Godfather" of San Diego who grew up in the city and is a longtime columnist for the *San Diego Tribune*, described the time he was first introduced to Ted: "Ted went to Hoover High, but given his address, he could have gone to either Hoover or San Diego." San Diego, of course, is where Canepa went. "So, the first thing I told Ted was: 'I've always been pissed at you.' In that booming voice he asks, 'Why?' I told him: 'Because I've always heard you didn't go to San Diego High because you didn't think you'd be good enough to play there.'" As Canepa relays, Ted confirmed that claim, something that makes him still "pissed."

Ted was plenty good enough that while at Hoover High, major league scouts had begun to notice him. In his senior-year Hoover yearbook, under Ted's photo there is just one word: "Baseball." The summer before his senior year, he traveled some 60 miles north to Fullerton to attend a St. Louis Cardinals camp. He was one of 350 kids trying out. Bothered by a sore leg from getting hit by a pitch the week before, he could barely run and he didn't hit all that well, either. There would be no Gashouse Gang for Ted Williams. One can only imagine how many more championships the Cardinals would have won during the next 20 years with both Williams and Stan Musial in the outfield. Oh my!

A scout from the New York Yankees was seriously interested in getting his name on a contract. The official story was his parents thought the signing money was too low, but also a factor was Ted was only 17 and his mother thought that was too young to be moving away from San Diego. Ted pretty much agreed—he was a tall, scrawny, green kid who hadn't really been anywhere. And, fortunately, to play pro ball at a higher level, he could stay home and play for the Padres.

The Pacific Coast League that Ted joined in 1936 had been offering West Coast fans high-quality baseball since 1903. That was one reason for its popularity by the mid-1930s, persisting through the woes of the Depression. Another was simply that it offered live professional baseball. At that time, the westernmost Major League Baseball team was the Cardinals, and St. Louis was almost 1,600 miles east of San Diego. And the highly partisan fans loved their home-team players, especially ones with more colorful names, such as Alan "Two Gun" Gettel, Tracie "Kewpie Dick" Barrett, Ernie "Bocce" Lombardi (the catcher was also called "the Schnozz"), "Lefty" O'Doul, "Jigger" Statz, "Ping" Bodie, and Carlos "the Comet" Bernier. For many players, the PCL was an immediate stepping-stone on their way up to the majors and a soft landing place on their way down.

The Padres ball club was new to San Diego. Technically, they went Hollywood because Hollywood went to San Diego. The Hollywood Stars, with Vincent DiMaggio, Frank Shellenback, and Cleo Carlyle included on the roster, had won more games from 1930 (when they won the pennant) to 1934 than any other PCL team. But the wheels fell off in 1935, with the Stars losing 99 games. Hollywood attendance plummeted, and the owner, Bill "Hardrock" Lane, faced a rent increase in order to continue sharing Wrigley Field with the Los Angeles Angels. In February 1936, the organization packed up and moved to San Diego, which by then had a population of 200,000. The newly christened Padres made their debut the following month at Lane Field, earning a victory over the Seattle Rainiers.

The high school teenager Ted Williams made his professional debut on June 27. In the second inning, he was sent up to pinch-hit for the pitcher Jack Hill. The hard-throwing righty Henry "Cotton" Pippen hurled three straight fastball strikes, and Ted's bat never left his shoulder because, he admitted, he was "petrified."

Ted finished the season with a decent .271 average, and the Padres made the playoffs. They had a young, talented outfield in Ted, Cedric Durst, and Vince DiMaggio, with another teenager, Bobby Doerr, at second base. They lost in five games, though, to the Oakland Oaks.

Ted's encounter with Lefty O'Doul was a pivotal experience. The older man had also advanced through the Pacific Coast League

and, like Ted, would concentrate on hitting at the expense of fielding. O'Doul was playing for the San Francisco Seals in 1927 when a
Chronicle columnist wrote about O'Doul, "He could run like a deer.
Unfortunately, he threw like one too." He began in the big leagues in
1928, and the following year, with the Philadelphia Athletics, he collected 254 hits and batted .398, an average that in the 90 years since
has been bettered only by Ted and Bill Terry. His 330 total of hits and
walks remains a National League record. When O'Doul retired after
the 1934 season, his career average was .349, behind only Ty Cobb,
Rogers Hornsby, and "Shoeless" Joe Jackson. Like Jackson, O'Doul
is not in the Hall of Fame. The reason: despite his obvious talent, he
played in only 970 games, 30 fewer than the minimum required. (If I
ever had a vote, both Lefty O'Doul and Shoeless Joe Jackson would
be in Cooperstown.)

One afternoon, the Seals were in San Diego for a series, and
O'Doul, by then the manager, got his first look at Ted during batting
practice. The astute hitting expert left the dugout and walked over to
him. "Kid," he said, "the best advice I can give you is don't let anybody
change you." Sage advice rendered, O'Doul returned to the dugout.
And Ted followed that advice in life as well as baseball.

During his two seasons in the Pacific Coast League, Ted was constantly trying to put on weight, routinely exceeding the $2.50 meal
allowance. Helping that effort was teammate Vince DiMaggio. "My
father taught Ted Williams how to eat," recalled his older daughter, Joanne DiMaggio Webber. "Ted had been just skin and bones
when he came to the Padres. My father would get him to eat better
for his strength, and of course he could feast when the Padres were in
San Francisco and my Grandmother Rosalie was cooking." Younger
brother Dominic would have met Ted at his parents' home four years
before they became teammates. Another younger brother, Joe, was
already in the majors.

During the 1937 season, Ted's best friend on the Padres was Hall
of Famer-to-be Bobby Doerr. He and the infielder were two of the
youngest members of the team, both liked fishing, and to kill time

on road trips they went to the theater to watch cowboy movies—the more westerns the better. There was a little friendly competition, too—who was going to make it to the majors first? During road trips to Portland, the two young men became friendly with the young clubhouse boy for the PCL Beavers, a home-grown product named Johnny Pesky, who had not yet impressed anyone as a potential major league player. "I certainly do remember John as the clubhouse boy," Dominic DiMaggio told Bill Nowlin for his biography of Pesky. "We'd come up to Portland and John was there and he took care of the clubhouse." (Not for long.)

Williams completed his second PCL season with a .291 average, 23 home runs, and 98 RBIs. Led by Williams and catcher George Detore (.334) and Jim Chaplin (23 victories), the Padres enjoyed an easy time in the playoffs. Williams got his club off to a fast start in the first game by going 4-for-5. The Padres swept Sacramento in the first round, then did the same to Portland and were handed the Governor's Cup.

After those personal and team accomplishments, destiny called. It was time to head to Boston and the major leagues.

***

After World War II ended and Americans were better able to travel, the Enbergs were on the move. We drove first to Michigan to visit my mother's family, then on to Minnesota to see my father's folks. While in Michigan, a real estate agent who was an old friend of my father showed him a 40-acre fruit farm on the outskirts of the small village of Armada. There was no agonizing decision to make—my father bought it. He wanted to be a farmer. Goodbye, Winnetka and Canoga Park and the valley, hello to the Midwest and its wicked winters. This caused some fretting: what would happen to my budding baseball career?

The transition was more complex than that. Our "new" home was a drafty, two-story wooden farmhouse that had been built during

Civil War times. Among the amenities it did not have were insulation in the walls, running water, central heating, and a bathroom. We did have a two-hole outhouse, a well that was dry from midsummer into November, and were within walking distance of a one-room school-house with only two other students in my class. We were asked to teach school children in the lower grades as an assist to the teacher. I believe that is where I first realized the nobility inherent in being an educator.

Everyone in the family—even my sister, Sharyl, was old enough to be part of it now—pitched in to work the farm. We grew a dozen varieties of apples, especially Red Delicious, the most popular. We also raised pears, plums, sour cherries, and sweet corn, and we made apple cider and collected honey. On weekends, I was the sole propri-etor of a small fruit stand on the edge of our farm. Of course, I could not imitate playing baseball games in winter, with the Michigan winds being brutally cold and sometimes up to three feet of snow on the ground, but I tried to make up for the lost time during the summer and fall weekends. On my portable radio I listened to Detroit Tigers games being broadcast by Van Patrick (who doubled as the Lions announcer in the fall), and when business was slow—it could be a couple of hours between cars stopping on the two-lane paved high-way between Armada and Mount Clemens—I took batting practice using rocks and an old, nicked-up bat.

My dream was not derailed; it simply had to be seasonally adjusted. In fact, one could say my situation improved because in the Tigers I had an MLB team to follow. (They had won a World Series as recently as 1945, thanks to great players like Hank Greenberg, Rudy York, Hal Newhouser, Dizzy Trout, and Virgil Trucks.) And thanks to the drama of that 1946 All-Star Game, I had Ted Williams to fol-low, who was at the peak of his career in the late 1940s. When the Red Sox were in Detroit, the rest of life didn't matter.

But sometimes life mattered a lot. As I would find out years later about Ted, my family also fractured. In the case of the Enbergs, it was my mother who left. She moved north to central Michigan and found work there. What happened between my parents left an indelible scar on myself and two siblings. When I entered Armada Rural Agricultural High School, sports beckoned—football and basketball as well as baseball. Being a star athlete—albeit being a big frog in a small pond—was within my grasp, and it was time to take the next step.

***

In December 1937, the Padres sold Ted Williams's contract to the Boston Red Sox. The deal worked out between Bill Lane and Eddie Collins, Boston's general manager, was that the Padres would get two players from the Red Sox system and $35,000, certainly a lot of money during the Depression. Ted read about the transaction in the newspaper and felt ill: "The Red Sox didn't mean a thing to me. A fifth-, sixth-place club, the farthest from San Diego I could go. Then Eddie Collins came to visit us."

Collins had first seen Ted hit the year before when he traveled west to scout and eventually sign Bobby Doerr. Because of Ted's age, Collins had to negotiate with his parents.

Years later, Collins would allow that he was miffed when during the visit to the Williams home on Utah Street, Ted never once stood up, whether to greet him or to say goodbye. He could not have known that the reason was the 19-year-old's shame over the house's condition. Collins was given the one decent chair to sit in, while Ted sat atop a towel that covered a huge hole in the other chair. Collins's displeasure did not prevent him from persuading the club's owner, Tom Yawkey, to okay a $1,000 signing bonus. Ted would soon be on a rocky path to Boston.

Part II

Baseball Adolescence with No Time for Acne

There is no tougher transition for a ballplayer than going from the minor leagues to what is called the "big show." For Ted Williams, a petulant teenager albeit already a mature hitter, there was an unusual transition that accompanied becoming a major leaguer—this San Diego kid had to go to Minnesota . . . and he ate it up (and almost everything else!).

His first stop, though, was Sarasota, Florida, where in 1938 the Boston Red Sox had their spring training camp—a big adventure for a 19-year-old who had never really gone anywhere outside San Diego and Southern California except where the Padres of the Pacific Coast League played. He was to travel across America by train. That spring, severe rainstorms in the Southwest washed away bridges and roads, causing delays for all travelers, so the Red Sox manager was already not too happy when Ted arrived late. The impudent young man inched further into Joe Cronin's doghouse when upon being introduced, he said, "Hiya, sport"—not exactly an acceptable greeting to a baseball authority figure. It was the first of many times Boston fans, sportswriters, and teammates would find Ted irrepressible. (Cronin, a future Hall of Famer and American League president, was only 31 yet beginning his sixth year as a manager as well as being the team's shortstop.) He would soon refer to the eccentric rookie as "Meat-head."

In his riveting *Summer of '49*, David Halberstam writes about Williams first coming to the Red Sox: "All he could talk about on that trip was how exciting this was, arriving at the very precipice of the major leagues, and how he hoped to be not just a major-leaguer but a great hitter. But to the veterans that spring, he seemed unbearably brash. He did not understand his own lowly position in the pecking order of a major-league team."

Ted silenced any criticism the best way he knew how—by hitting. That first morning in camp, Ted was told to take batting practice against the pitching coach. This was not just another coach, but Herb Pennock, a Hall of Fame hurler who had starred for the Philadelphia Athletics, Red Sox, and Yankees for 23 seasons. Ted easily pulled the ball, sending line drives to right. When he stepped out of the box, he realized everyone on the field and in the stands had watched in hushed silence.

It was also on that first day that Ted acquired one of his most famous nicknames. Because he was a late arrival, he was greeted with, "Where you been, Kid?" This came from Johnny Orlando, who would be the Red Sox equipment manager for decades and become one of Ted's best friends. From that moment on, Orlando and eventually millions of others would refer to Ted Williams as the Kid. It was not his favorite nickname . . . he preferred "Teddy Ballgame."

He had a friendly face in camp in Bobby Doerr, his former Padres teammate. He was just four months older than Ted yet was beginning his second season with the Red Sox. Another former Padre was Vince DiMaggio (older brother to Joe and Dominic), whom Ted greeted before an exhibition game against the Boston Bees, the major league club that had purchased DiMaggio's contract the year before.

Early in spring training, Ted continued to impress with his hitting but became the subject of head-scratching headlines because of his indifferent fielding— which included shouting, "Hi-yo, Silver, away!"

like the Lone Ranger when he galloped after fly balls. There were also frequent, spontaneous outbursts to himself and to others that only occasionally made sense. The initial impression at the Sarasota camp was that "the Kid" needed to grow up.

Ted needed more seasoning, and the Red Sox offered that to him less than two weeks later by giving him a bus ticket to Daytona Beach, where he would join their top minor league affiliate, the Minneapolis Millers. As Ted was leaving camp, the defiant side of him emerged. He was getting a good ribbing from Ben Chapman, Doc Cramer, and Joe Vosmik, the starting outfield for the Red Sox. Ted shouted, "I'll be back and I'll make more money in one year than the three of you combined!" The older players, who may have earned as much as $15,000 each in 1938, got a good laugh out of the declaration then. In 1946, after Ted returned from three years in the military, the prediction was proved true, with $5000 to spare, when Boston gave him a $50,000 contract. On that March day, however, Orlando had to loan Ted $5 to buy food for the bus trip.

He made an immediate impression in Daytona Beach—though again, not quite the right one. Ted got off the bus and spotted a Western Union messenger. He borrowed the boy's bicycle and rode it around the bus station shouting out salutations and introducing himself. As Ben Bradlee Jr. noted in his book, Ted became known as a "screwball."

Nevertheless, with the Minneapolis club, Ted got lucky in two ways—one was his manager, Donnie Bush, who patiently endured the uncommon antics of the aggravating but supremely talented youngster, more than any minor league manager should have to. The other way was, during that season Ted came to love Minnesota.

Bush had been a good fielding, no hitting shortstop in the majors and then became a manager, with the Chicago White Sox and Washington Senators on his résumé. His one World Series appearance was with the Pittsburgh Pirates, where he had the misfortune to go up against Miller Huggins and his omnipotent 1927 Yankees. With the Red Sox organization, his primary role was to ready the club's top prospects for the big show. In Ted Williams, he faced a huge talent, a confident kid in a man's body in a baseball sense; yet on the other hand, a frightened, unpredictable, insecure teenager far from home. At one point in that season, Bush told the club's owner, Mike Kelly, "It's Williams or me, one has to go." Fortunately, the manager withdrew that statement, because the Red Sox were not about to cut such potential loose . . . and like he often did, Ted began to grow on him a bit, then a lot.

Minnesota provided Ted the opportunity to exercise his two loves. When he wasn't at the ballpark, he was fishing in the land of 10,000 lakes. When he was at the ballpark, he was busy wearing out right field, while punishing pitching staffs comprised of young players on their way up and grizzled veterans on their way down. By the end of the AAA season, Ted had accumulated a stunning .366 average with 46 home runs and 142 RBIs. He had just turned 20. Oh my! There was no doubt that Ted Williams would be part of Beantown baseball the next year. The Red Sox had to make room for such an incredible talent.

Most of all, for the good and the bad, there was Ted's all-consuming emphasis on hitting. As awed as Donnie Bush could sometimes be with the youngster's batting, his job was to mold a complete ballplayer. Ted wasn't on the same page. With the Minneapolis club he played right field, and one afternoon he took his position without his sunglasses. Sure enough, an opponent hit one at him and Ted lost it in the sun.

After two runs had scored, a furious Bush raced out to right field and screamed, "Where the hell are your glasses?"

"I forgot 'em, Skip."

"Well go in there and get them!" As Ted recalled, "It was like me in those days to say, 'Why does he take everything so seriously?'"

While Rogers Hornsby was not the idol that Bill Terry had been, Ted had great respect for the man who finished second to Ty Cobb's lifetime .366 with a .358 batting average. (Ted told me years later that he regarded Hornsby as the greatest right-handed hitter in the history of the game.) "The Rajah" had retired from the lowly St. Louis Browns as a player-manager the year before—at age 42, he hit .321!—and while serving as a part-time hitting instructor with the Millers, he took an interest in Ted: "I liked Hornsby because he talked to me, a kid of nineteen, and boy I picked his brains for everything I could." Something Hornsby told him stuck with Ted: "Get a good ball to hit." Ted was a good student. No wonder he would average fewer than fifty strikeouts a season and routinely lead the American League in walks.

While the Minneapolis club finished only in sixth place, though above .500 at 78-74, its right fielder earned the AAA triple crown. To be fair to AAA pitchers, the porch in right field at Nicolett Park in Minneapolis was only 279 feet from home, not unlike the distance at the ballpark around the corner from his house in North Park, San Diego. (This turned out to be good preparation for playing in his favorite hitting park, Briggs Stadium in Detroit. More on that later.) Still, no matter how good the Red Sox outfield was, Ted would have to be shoehorned somewhere the next season.

***

At the same age as Ted when he was attending Hoover High in San Diego, I was pursuing my own dreams of athletic glory with the Armada (Michigan) High School Tigers. Making such heights a lot harder to scale was that as a freshman I weighed just 95 pounds and stood barely five feet tall. During that year and the next one, the best I could do was play on the junior varsity teams and ride the pine on the varsity level. Still, I strove to be a multisport athlete by trying my best in football and basketball as well as baseball. Away from school and working at our farm's fruit stand, I continued to narrate my achievements as I socked rocks over the telephone wires across the road. Becoming a star was only a matter of time.

Finally, toward the end of my sophomore year, I began to grow. It was a heck of a surge, too—an inch a month for five months. Though not as dramatically, I continued to add height and weight and was closing in on six feet during my senior year, when I was the quarterback on the football team, starting pitcher on the baseball team, and captain and center of the basketball squad—probably one of the shortest centers on any Michigan hoops team. Yet there was no one taller on our small farm team. I fouled out of every game. At least they couldn't exile me to Daytona Beach!

To continue to play sports in college—in fact, to go to college at all—would take some luck. My grades had allowed me to finish third of 33 students in the 1952 Armada Agricultural High School graduating class. My family joined the many in our rural farm area who could not afford to send their kid to college. But at the graduation ceremony that June, Dr. Charles Anspach, the president of what was then the Central Michigan College of Education, gave the commencement address. I was impressed by him, but more important, my mother was now working on that campus, and when I nervously approached and mentioned this, Dr. Anspach said he knew her. Despite a solid academic record, I had no plans to continue my education. He suggested my principal send my grades to him.

My principal came through, and three weeks later a letter arrived informing me I had been accepted for admission and I was to receive a $100 academic scholarship. They're going to *pay me* to go to college? So that September, off I went, hitchhiking to college . . . and there, my athletic dreams died. No longer a big fish in a small pond, I was outshone on every team. My college athletic résumé would forever read: Junior Varsity. During my sophomore year, the only varsity competition for which I qualified was the debate team. In this, I had again been lucky. This was an excellent educational experience, as I learned—as if all those afternoons at the fruit stand hadn't taught me enough—that I could talk a better game than I played.

Alas, that summer, despite taking on any job I could find and even with the scholarship ($100 went further then!), the arithmetic told me after two years that I couldn't afford to continue at Central Michigan. I went to work on an assembly line putting front bumpers on the 1955 Dodge at a plant in Hamtramck, outside Detroit. The work was hard, but it paid pretty well (over $2 an hour!), and thankfully a lot of people were buying Dodge cars and trucks. By the following January, feeling very grateful, I was back happily at the Central campus.

I soon had even more for which to be grateful. A fellow member of the debate team, who was graduating, promoted me for the job of replacing him as the public address announcer for Central Michigan football and basketball games. Oh my, this position paid $3 a game! I spent my junior and senior years behind the microphone. Oddly, this wasn't the doorway to a broadcasting career. That doorway was not with a microphone, but with a broom in my hands.

***

The Minnesota fans would be sorry to see Ted go. The brash kid with the infectious smile and Paul Bunyan-like hitting feats had totally charmed them. *The Kid* includes this excerpt from a *Minneapolis Journal* sports column published during the 1938 season: "There was not a fan in the park who did not form an immediate attachment to gangling Ted. He is as loose as red flannels in a clothes line, but as beautifully coordinated as a fine watch when he tenses for action. He is six feet and several inches of athlete and the same number of feet and inches in likeable boyishness."

Ted was in no hurry to return to the unhappy home life awaiting him in San Diego, but he had purchased a Buick convertible in Minneapolis that he knew would impress the North Park neighbors. After a two-week barnstorming tour with several teammates, he drove to California. There he learned that the Red Sox were not going to further delay Ted's major league debut. Even though Ben Chapman had hit .340 the year before, he was sent packing by Boston to the Cleveland Indians, opening up right field and the uniform number 9. Ted felt flattered by that big vote of confidence, and he set off in the Buick for Sarasota eager to be a major leaguer. He was accompanied by Les Cassie, who had acted as a sort of surrogate father to Ted, attending some of his games and teaching him how to fish. When he had graduated from

Hoover High, the fountain pen Cassie had given him was Ted's only present.

He apparently hadn't learned much the previous year about addressing Cronin. This time, his greeting was, "Hi, Joe, how's the old boy?" He was full of energy and ambition and, as ever, full of himself. "That spring I was a nuisance to everybody," while in camp, "asking [Jimmie] Foxx and Cronin and Cramer and Vosmik about this pitcher or that one. I quizzed every player on the team, and they all had something to say." At an early age, despite his cocky and at times obnoxious manner, Ted was always eager to learn. Whether baseball or, later, world affairs, he was on a path to perfection, and the more he knew, the better he could reach that goal.

He had filled out to 6'4" and 175 pounds—a "splendid splinter" indeed—and being still only 20 years old, he would only get stronger. (Ted took Johnny Orlando's advice and drank buttermilk after every practice.) When he wasn't hitting, shagging flies, and otherwise preparing for his rookie season, Ted was at the movies. Westerns were his passion, and not surprisingly, John Wayne, who after years of B movies would break through that year in *Stagecoach*, became his favorite. In future years, for kids like me, Ted Williams and John Wayne were interchangeable. Some say he was John Wayne before John Wayne, though the actor was 11 years older. Apparently, it wasn't easy watching a movie with Ted in the audience, as he couldn't help talking back to some of the actors up on the screen.

The opening game of the 1939 season was in New York. This would not only be Ted's first regular-season matchup with the man who would be his chief rival the next 13 years, Joe DiMaggio, but Lou Gehrig was also still on the club. Like everyone else, Ted was unaware that a fatal illness was already taking its toll on the Iron Man. As he had in his Pacific Coast League debut, in his first major league at-bat, against Red Ruffing, he was out on three straight strikes. (He finished the game 1-for-4.)

Boston's home opener that April was the first time Ted saw Fenway Park. It felt especially good to greet the Boston fans with a double, a home run, and a triple. Icing on the cake was the fact that his first two hits were off Cotton Pippen, the same hurler who struck Ted out looking his first time up as a professional with the Padres. By the way, Bill Lane, the owner of the San Diego club, did not have the opportunity to see Ted play major league baseball. In October 1938, right after Ted completed his first season with the Minneapolis Millers, Lane died at 78.

Ted's first season with the Red Sox was a record-setting blockbuster. In July he was hitting a respectable .280 but didn't make the All-Star team, and then he got hot, especially collecting RBIs. The potent Boston lineup had Ted batting behind Cramer, Vosmik, and Foxx, and followed by Cronin, fellow Minneapolis alum Jim Tabor, and Bobby Doerr. The first three men got on base a lot, and back then, pitchers preferred to face Ted rather than the veteran Cronin. Williams wound up hitting .327, but more important, "the Kid" became the first rookie to lead the American League in runs batted in—with 143, a record that stands to this day.

One of his other accomplishments was to hit a ball out of Briggs Stadium in Detroit. Years later, that stadium became a home away from home for me to watch my hero . . . to cheer him, and maybe, maybe, to get to meet him.

***

Thank goodness Ted Williams loved to walk everywhere. Maybe he had no choice, with all that restless energy bursting to get out between games.

Okay, let me explain. It was thanks to Ted's penchant for walking rather than taking taxis that allowed me as a high-schooler to get as close as I dared to the Kid. And thanks also go to dear old Briggs Stadium, once home of the Detroit Tigers.

Ted had made his debut there during his 1939 rookie season, on May 4, and showed right away why it would become his favorite ballpark in which to hit. The right field foul pole was 325 feet away, to double-decked bleachers. His second time up that afternoon, Ted hit a ball that struck the top of roof. Not satisfied with that, his next time up, the ball went up over the roof and completely out of the park. It landed on Trumbull Avenue, took a bounce, and hit a taxi garage on the other side of the street. Years later, I asked Ted that if the Red Sox had traded him to Detroit and he played 77 home games there, how many home runs did he think he would hit in any given season. Without a moment's hesitation, he barked, "Eighty!" (Oh, wouldn't it be something to be Ted Williams!)

By that time, I was a student at Armada High, and Ted had been my hero for several years. Even though Armada and Detroit were 40 miles apart, I considered myself pretty lucky. In what was then an eight-team American League, even with a shorter 154-game season, the Red Sox would play the Tigers several series a year. In 1950, for example, the Red Sox played 14 games at Briggs Stadium. Sure, I'd have been better off living 40 miles from Fenway Park, but with my hero I didn't think about what I didn't have, only what I had—and that was the opportunity to see Ted Williams in his favorite hitting park. And oh what a show he would put on during batting practice! To watch him practice was to listen to Arthur Rubinstein rehearse on the piano, never producing a sour note, only sweet music.

What about television? The first baseball game broadcast on TV was in August 1939, the Cincinnati Reds against the Dodgers at Ebbets Field in Brooklyn. With a world war in between, baseball on television had not come very far by the end of the 1940s, and most people (like my family) couldn't afford a set anyway. This wasn't necessarily a drawback at all. With Ted, because of the absence of visual images, my imagination made him all the bigger. In fact, he was bigger than life itself. While writing this book, I asked Vin Scully, the legendary Dodgers broadcaster, about this, and he responded, "It was an advantage for those of us in that era to be influenced more strongly by black-and-white radio. Our imaginations added the bold, creative colors." (By the way, though living in the Bronx, Scully's boyhood idol was also a home run-hitting left-handed batter, Mel Ott of the New York Giants.)

In many homes, including my own, the radio was our "entertainment center," converting the living room into a "media room." A favorite of mine was a national show called *Cavalcade of Sports*, hosted by Bill Stern, on Friday nights. He would have writers manufacture heroic stories about Babe Ruth, James Stewart, the Pope, and others. Who was I to question their validity? I devoured those stories as true, totally inspired.

Still, as stimulating as radio could be, the fact was that if I wanted to actually see my hero Ted Williams in the flesh, it had to be at Briggs Stadium.

My high school catcher, Dave Dunham, and I hitchhiked to Detroit. During the games we rooted for our beloved Tigers, but before the umpire bellowed, "Play ball!" we were certain to be in the stands to watch Ted take batting practice. This was to witness a virtuoso in action, a master craftsman expressing himself better than anyone in the history of baseball. He never wavered from his belief that the most difficult feat in all of sport was "to hit a round ball with a round bat, squarely." To see Ted Williams take batting practice, especially in an arena where he so enjoyed performing, was a spectacle worth *crawling* the 80 miles round-trip.

He never took a bad swing. He rarely fouled the ball off or hit a ground ball. It was just line drive after line drive after line drive. There was the same routine before every game—his first round of swings was to rip the ball to right field, then he switched to driving the ball into the lower deck in right. At Briggs Stadium, there was only a short gap between the upper-deck overhang and the fence on top of the base of the right-field wall. He smashed the ball into that small gap with the ease of a champion golfer driving 1-irons. The concluding round of practice brought the anticipation and raw excitement of watching him try to hit the ball deep into the upper deck or even over the roof.

It could be great fun outside Briggs Stadium, too. When in town, the Red Sox stayed at the Book-Cadillac Hotel in downtown Detroit. It was a mile from the park, but when the weather was good, Ted and some teammates would walk to it down Michigan Avenue. My friend Dave (now a retired U.S. Army colonel) and I would position ourselves across the street to watch the players emerge, well-dressed men wearing identity-revealing "give-away" wing-tip shoes. One day, Ted Williams and his manager, Steve O'Neill, stepped out of the hotel.

We followed them all the way down Michigan Avenue. We were something out of a Bowery Boys movie, amateur detectives—when they slowed down, we slowed down; when they stopped, we stopped; when they resumed walking, we hurried to catch up. As full of joy and excitement as this experience was, I was too in awe to actually ask my hero for a handshake, or even an autograph. It was like mission accomplished when we saw Ted and O'Neill disappear into the ballpark's players' entrance. I wanted to shout to the heavens that I had been *that close* to touching my baseball god.

***

When his rookie season in Boston ended, Ted opted for a North Country winter rather than return home to San Diego. It wasn't just the lure of hunting and fishing, but also, as Ted admitted in his autobiography, his home life wasn't all rosy. Plus, there was a girl—later to be wife—involved, by the name of Doris Soule. While there, he lived in a room at the King Cole Hotel in downtown Minneapolis. Allowed to use the indoor batting cage at the University of Minnesota, he kept himself in baseball shape.

The 1940 season was a tough one for Ted, even though there would be an important and positive addition for the Red Sox and him personally. After batting .360 with 239 hits with the San Francisco Seals, Dominic DiMaggio made the leap directly from the Pacific Coast League to Boston. He would be the third player of the Red Sox version of the "core four," with Ted and Doerr and Johnny Pesky (in

1942), who would help deliver the best sequence of seasons ever for the Red Sox until the first decade of the 21st century. "Dommie," as Ted called him, would be Boston's leadoff batter, and with Pesky batting second, they were constantly scampering home as Ted's RBI total mounted. Just as important, not just during Ted's career but for the rest of his life, was the strong friendship he had with Joe's kid brother.

Nor did Ted have to suffer through a "sophomore slump"—in most categories, his 1940 season was as strong as his rookie year. But it was a tough year because his bitter battles with the Boston press began. One catalyst occurred after Ted had had a bad day against the Cleveland Indians, and a reporter overheard Ted vent, "Nuts to this baseball. I'd sooner be a fireman." The newspapers scoffed that this brash ballplayer proclaimed he'd rather fight fires for a few hundred dollars a month than hit baseballs for better pay. Ted took a lot of ridicule for that, with opposing players wearing Texaco fire hats and blowing sirens in their dugouts.

Still just a kid, Ted didn't know how to defuse such situations. And as the Boston press, sensing blood in the water, wrote increasingly critical articles about the 21-year-old, Ted decided to counter with anger toward the reporters.

Ben Bradlee Jr. contends that because the reporters for the eight major daily newspapers in Boston were no longer giving him a rookie pass and were critical of him with increasing frequency, it had an adverse effect on Ted and his relationships with writers, teammates, and fans. It didn't help that later in the season Ted told a reporter he wouldn't object to a trade away from Boston: "I know I'd be a hero in Brooklyn."

There were some on-the-field challenges, too. First, the good news: Ted was switched to left field, which meant not as much Fenway Park real estate to roam, and Tom Yawkey had installed a bullpen in right field, causing the fence to be moved in to a more batter-friendly distance of 380 feet (yet still a home-run challenge). Fans gave it the nickname Williamsburg because they expected Ted, especially, would take advantage of the closer porch. But in 1940, Jimmie

Foxx and Joe Cronin would turn 33 and 34, respectively, and their offensive abilities were waning. As a result, Ted found pitchers reluctant to give him a good pitch to hit. They were more likely to walk him and take their chances with the aging stars behind him in the lineup. Cronin addressed this by switching Williams and Foxx, making Ted the clean-up hitter, but the result was his home run and RBI totals were down (though he led the league in runs scored). The smarter pitchers had a full year of experience with Ted, and during the 1940 season, they adjusted their approaches accordingly.

Ted, though, believed that he was as smart as any pitcher. His strong 1940 stats and his .344 lifetime average proved he was right. He even had success on the mound.

During one game, when the Tigers were beating Boston 11-1 in the seventh inning in Detroit and Cronin put him on the mound as an emergency reliever, to eat up a couple of innings in a blowout game, Ted tossed two innings and struck out one of the home team's best hitters (and future teammate), Rudy York. Though I was too young to see or listen to this game (and I was still in the San Fernando Valley anyway), Ted's only major league pitching performance would be a very important one for me, as well as for Ted . . . which I'll get to a little later.

The Red Sox with 82 wins finished 10 games over .500, but that was good for only fifth place that year. In the off-season, it was back to Minnesota, and Doris, and hunting and fishing for Ted. While he always had confidence in his abilities—his oft-stated goal during his career was that people who see him would remark, "There goes Ted Williams, the greatest hitter of all time"—he still could not have expected that the next season would be the most spectacular one of his life.

For anyone who loved baseball—and in those prewar seasons, it was *the* most popular sport in America, followed by boxing and horse racing—the 1941 season was like Christmas every day. In the National League, the Brooklyn Dodgers, who had been dubbed "Dem

Bums" two years earlier, earned their first pennant in 21 years. It was a great season in general for major league offense—as an example, a shortstop with the Washington Senators named Cecil Travis hit .359, then never hit higher than .252. But in all of baseball, most eyes were on the exploits of the Yankee Clipper and the Kid.

Entire forests have been felled to provide paper to write about Joe DiMaggio's 56-game hitting streak. Immediately, it was regarded, along with other incredible records like Babe Ruth's 714 home runs and Lou Gehrig's 2,130 consecutive games played, as a record that would never be equaled, let alone broken. DiMaggio's has proven to be the more enduring feat. As impressive as Ted batting .406 was at the time, it has taken longer to fully appreciate it. For one thing, in the 65 years of major league baseball previous to 1941, an average of .400 or more had been achieved 27 times, with the most recent being 11 years earlier, when Bill Terry of the New York Giants batted .401. But in the 77 years since Ted in 1941 (as of this writing), *no one* has achieved .400. The closest was .394 by Tony Gwynn, coincidentally of the San Diego Padres. Next was Rod Carew, another left-handed hitter, in 1977 with .388, the same Ted hit in 1957 . . . when he was 39 years old!

The season did not begin all that well for Ted. In spring training, while sliding into second base, he suffered a chipped bone in his right ankle. The best he could offer the rest of the exhibition season, once he could at least limp up to the plate, was pinch-hit. But Bobby Doerr, who by then knew Ted better than anyone on the team, saw a silver lining in that the ankle injury. It caused an alteration in Ted's swing so that he would make even better contact with the ball. And, by not playing much, Ted would be even more eager than usual to get out on the field when he was sufficiently healed.

Doerr must've been right because when the actual season began, it was like a recuperated Ted was launched out of a cannon. He hit over .300 during April, then in May he truly took off, finishing the month at .436. On May 15, DiMaggio began his hitting streak. Ted did too, one that lasted until June 8, and during it he batted .487. With walks included, Ted had reached base more than half the times he strode to the plate. During DiMaggio's entire record-smashing streak, he hit an astounding .408 . . . and Ted batted .412 during those same 56 games.

Whether or not Ted did hit .400 or Boston wound up in the World Series (alas, the team finished second to the Yankees, at 84-70), he would at least have to treasure always what he called "the most thrilling hit of my life." That came in the 1941 All-Star Game. Held at Briggs Stadium, there were five Red Sox representatives—starters Joe Cronin, Bobby Doerr, and Ted, and reserves Jimmie Foxx and Dom DiMaggio, who shared the stage with his brother Joe. But it was Ted who took the rousing final bow.

Though Ted doubled to drive in a run in the fourth inning, it looked like Arky Vaughan of the Pittsburgh Pirates would grab the headlines in the late editions of the July 8 newspapers. (Like most baseball games then, the All-Star Game was played during the day.) Vaughan had slugged two home runs, and the National League held a 5-3 advantage going into the bottom of the ninth inning. When the catcher Frankie Hayes of the Philadelphia Athletics popped out, the junior circuit's chances became even slimmer.

But Ken Keltner of the Cleveland Indians legged out an infield hit. (A few weeks later, the third baseman's brilliant defense would end Joe DiMaggio's bid for a 57-game hitting streak.) Joe Gordon of the Yankees singled, and Cecil Travis walked. The bases were loaded. The Yankee Clipper hit the ball hard . . . but it was a perfect double-play ball. The game continued, however, when Billy Herman's throw to first went wide and Keltner scored to make it 5-4. Two outs, runners at the corners, and young Ted Williams at the plate. On a 2-and-1 pitch, he blasted the ball off the third tier of the right-field stands and it landed back on the field. Outfielder Enos Slaughter, who would torment the Red Sox in the 1946 World Series, pocketed the ball and loped toward the dugout.

Ted would refer to that moment as a dream. Oh my, doesn't that sound familiar to many of us! A walk-off homer to win the All-Star Game is one of the best dreams a baseball-loving kid can have, and the ultimate Kid had just made it come true. There was no mistaking his youthful joy and exuberance—the fans screamed as the Kid rounded the bases, laughing and clapping and galloping like a young colt. Only over time would we come to realize Ted, perhaps rivaled only by Joe DiMaggio, had a robust flair for the dramatic moment. Teammates rushed him as he crossed the plate, clapping his strong shoulders and back, mussing his hair, and Del Baker, the Tigers manager, even kissed him. Probably no one was more effusive than Artie Fletcher, the Yankees pitching coach, who shook Ted's hand 12 times.

Afterward, Ted celebrated with an extra-large chocolate milkshake. He was further buoyed by a telegram from his mom, May, congratulating him for being on the All-Star team, and learning his mother had listened to the game on the radio.

Aside from his on-field achievements, what was especially gratifying to Ted—and an indication of how much others in the league thought of the Kid (who would turn only 23 that August)—was that as Ted continued to pound the ball, around the league players began rooting for him to break that .400 barrier. One example was the four-time batting champion Harry Heilmann, who preceded Van Patrick as the Tigers radio play-by-play announcer and, more importantly, as a Detroit player had finished the 1921 season with a .403 average. One afternoon at Briggs Stadium when the Red Sox were in town, Heilmann took Ted aside and said, "Now, forget about that short fence, just hit the ball where you want it, hit your pitch, get those base hits. You can hit .400. You can do it." There was support even at Yankee Stadium. Ted had gotten three hits off Lefty Gomez, and the fourth time up when he walked Ted, Lefty's own fans booed him.

For the first time, an opposing team tried a shift, putting three infielders on the right side. The White Sox strategy lasted just two games, with Ted going 4-for-10, including a double to left. On his birthday on August 30, his average was .407.

His highest average in September was .413, before it began to drop. His bat cooled with the temperature. With two days left in the season, a doubleheader against the Athletics, his average was .39955, which rounded off to .400. Any ballplayer then or now (see Colorado's D.J. Lemahieu's 2016 N.L. battling title) who sat out the last two games to preserve what was a once-in-a-generation—heck, once in a lifetime!—accomplishment would not have been blamed, and maybe even patted on the back for not being such a hardhead. Instead, this would be another example of Ted's unquestioned integrity. When Joe Cronin suggested sitting, Ted responded, "I want to play it out. I want to play it all the way." He wasn't about to hit .400 sitting on the bench.

That night, Ted did wrestle with his decision a bit. His big, strong body was churning with more than its usual quota of restless energy. He walked for miles and miles through the streets of Philadelphia, accompanied by the faithful Johnny Orlando. The latter wasn't keen on so much exercise, so for every time Ted stopped to buy ice cream, Orlando darted into a different establishment to drain a shot of scotch.

They could have rested their legs and liver, respectively, because Saturday's game was rained out. The mountain to climb had grown taller—a Sunday afternoon double-header at damp and chilly Shibe Park. His first time up, as he dug in, the Philadelphia catcher, Frankie Hayes, told Ted that the manager, Connie Mack, had warned his team that anyone who lets up on Williams would be run out of baseball. "I wish you all the luck in the world," the catcher said, "but we're not giving you a damn thing."

That turned out to be okay, because Ted came out swinging. In the first game, he singled, homered, and singled twice more. He had two more hits in the second game, and the day's total was 6-for-8. Ted had not just safely clung to .400, but surpassed it easily, finishing at .406. He also led the American League in home runs, runs scored, walks, and slugging percentage. His 120 RBIs were five short of DiMaggio's total, or he would have earned the Triple Crown. (Even more impressive: at that time, sacrifice flies were counted as at-bats; with today's rule, Ted would have batted .411.)

In any other season, Teddy Ballgame would have been the hands-down Most Valuable Player. But the award went to Joe DiMaggio. Even Ted agreed with the voters of the Baseball Writers Association of America and their 291-254 tally. Joe had that 56-game hitting streak—many people don't know that after it was broken in Cleveland, he had an additional 19-game streak—and the Yankees won the pennant. Ted was four years younger than Joe, and his turn would come.

During that fall, the possibility that the United States would be drawn into the war in Europe grew stronger every day. In November, Ted visited his draft board and was classified III-A because he was his mother's sole source of income. (Unofficially, for the most part so was his brother, Danny, who had regular brushes with the law and did not hold jobs for long.) On December 7, Ted was at a hotel in Minnesota, just back from a hunting trip, when he heard on the radio the Japanese had attacked Pearl Harbor. Within 48 hours, Cleveland's pitching ace Bob Feller had enlisted and would miss the next four seasons while serving in the Navy, and other players signed up too, but not Ted, who was absorbed by his own issues.

The US government eagerly got "concerned" for him. He was reclassified I-A, which meant be ready to pack a bag. But Ted's first battle was against the Selective Service. He hired a lawyer and appealed the decision. Given that his father had not given May a dime in many years, her focus on saving souls instead of money, and Danny's troubles, Ted had a legitimate case. (In a case of unfortunate timing for Ted, his parents had just finalized their divorce.) Without the Red Sox salary, his mother could wind up in the street next to the men to whom she preached. But during that fervently patriotic, post-Pearl Harbor period, the press came down hard on Ted. And Quaker Oats cancelled its endorsement contract with him.

With the matter unresolved when 1942 spring training began, Ted reported to Sarasota, consoled with a $30,000 contract. Still, it was a tough season because he was bitter about his parents' divorce and heightened criticism from fans. (One letter he received was nothing more than a blank sheet of yellow paper.) All Ted did was win the Triple Crown—36 home runs, 137 RBIs, and a .356 average, and with 141 he also led the American League in runs scored.

This time with the MVP voting, Ted had a legitimate beef. Incredibly, the award went to Yankees second baseman Joe Gordon, whose stat line was .322, 18 homers, 103 RBIs. The voting was 270-249. Clearly, Ted's ongoing problems with the press had cost him votes, even allowing that Gordon had helped New York to return to the Fall Classic. Ted was unusually gracious about the slight.

Quietly, earlier in the season, Ted enlisted in the Navy, requesting aviation. He was called up in November, and with Joe Coleman of the Athletics and Johnny Pesky, coming off his rookie season with the Red Sox, he went to training at Amherst College. In *The Teammates*, David Halberstam would quote Pesky about Ted: "It was like there was a star on the top of his head, pulling everyone toward him, like a beacon. He was special in some marvelous way and we were that more special because we played with him." Now they would be playing for Uncle Sam.

In the waning days of 1942, he was no more special than any other soldier or sailor. For the first time—but not the last—Ted Williams went to war.

Part III
War and Play

As a freshman at Central Michigan during the Korean War, the closest I came to active duty was joining the US Naval Reserve. The expectation was I would finish college as a reserve, do two years of required active duty, then complete the six-year reservist commitment. But there would be no Ted-like induction for me, because before I graduated, the war ended (via a truce, not a treaty) and the American military was downsizing. Okay, then, time to get a job and prepare for a career. I had majored in health and physical education and planned to be a high school P.E. teacher and coach.

But before graduation, the job I got was as a janitor. And that was where my broadcasting career really began. As I've heard my friend John McEnroe say many times, "You can't be serious," but indeed I am.

Chuck Miller was a Phi Sig fraternity brother in his last year at Central Michigan and thus no longer would need an off-campus janitor position. I was interested because it paid a dollar an hour, and I had been pulling a grand sum of 60 cents per hour busing trays in the dormitory. The job was at WCEN in Mount Pleasant, the only radio or television station in the entire midstate area surrounding the college campus. I had worked a summer at a Chrysler plant in Detroit as a custodian, so I knew my way in and around a broom closet. Plus, how dirty could a small radio station known as the "Pleasant Voice of Michigan" get?

I showed up for my interview all set to start sweeping. I'd never stepped into a radio station. But Russ Holcomb, the general manager, told me WCEN also needed a weekend disc jockey and wanted me to audition—right then and there. There was nothing to do but wing it by reading a five-minute newscast and two 60-second commercials. When I left, I was less concerned about blowing what I felt was an awkward audition than missing out on the janitor job. Holcomb decided I would be a better announcer than custodian and offered me the weekend job as a DJ. My eyes brightened at the thought of even bigger bucks. But it was not to be—the DJ job also paid a dollar an hour. Apparently, quality was not a major requirement.

The broadcasting industry is littered with the short-lived careers of part-time and weekend show hosts who for various reasons never took another step forward. Talent helps, sure, and hard work, of course, but sometimes it boils down to luck. I had barely settled in at WCEN when the station's sports director had a dispute with management and he found the exit. Well, I was never going to realize my dreams as a baseball star, but I knew enough about those who were, and I wasted no time accepting the job.

Then the hard work part really began. I'd be the play-by-play voice of the Central Michigan football and basketball games and do the play-by-play of two high schools' teams plus writing and offering a nightly 15-minute sports report, all while still going to school—and all at $1 an hour. On holidays like Thanksgiving and Christmas I worked 16-hour shifts, because no one else wanted to work on the holiday. I had no hesitation signing on and signing off and earning $16 a day playing holiday music. Then even before I graduated, WSAM Radio in Saginaw hired me to work weekends for $2 an hour, and for a full summer as a replacement for news and other disc jockeys during their vacations. WCEN wouldn't come close to paying that, even after I offered a hometown discount.

Off I went to the "bigger" radio station to the southeast. I really felt I was on my way. Who knows, I'd never hit like my hero, but maybe the day would come when I'd broadcast a game that had Ted Williams in the line-up. I was 21 and still dreaming.

***

To be in the Navy was never a dream of Ted's. He had no choice. Leigh Montville reports in his book *Ted Williams: The Biography of An American Hero* that when he had been first inducted into the Navy, the military doctor testing Ted's vision claimed he was one of four or five out of 100 who could see better than 20-20. In fact, there are reports that Ted tested 20-15 vision. In other words, Ted would see a ball in full focus for the complete 60-foot distance, when a batter with so-called "perfect 20-20 vision" wouldn't see it that clearly until the ball was 45 feet from the plate. Argue as Ted might, this was a tremendous advantage. And if he was 20-12, as some have surmised, it means that his vision was literally off the charts, allowing Ted to see the ball clearly (such as if it has any spin to it) from the moment it leaves the pitcher's hand. Oh my!

In his book *Ted Williams at War*, Bill Nowlin includes this recollection from Lew Powers, a fellow cadet who lived in Massachusetts but still couldn't afford to make the trip home for Christmas: "I bumped into Williams in the fraternity house where the cadets were living. He asked me in that big bluff way of his: 'No home to go to?' I just passed it off, something to the effect I was broke and let it go at that. He wouldn't let go. He forced money into my hand, a couple of hundred dollars, and told me in no uncertain terms to get the hell out of there."

He didn't stay at Amherst too long because the next stop for aviation training was Chapel Hill, North Carolina. During his time there, Ted briefly encountered another cadet, and a college baseball player, George Herbert Walker Bush. They would not get to know each other until 45 years later, in 1988, when Ted would be seriously active in helping the ex-Yale first baseman to the office of President of the United States.

The military base had a baseball team called the Cloudbusters, and Ted and Johnny Pesky joined it. The exhibition games served the purpose of getting in some practice, as no one knew how long the war would last and when the major leaguers would be back with their respective teams. The practice came in handy when suddenly Ted was back in Boston, playing at Fenway Park. Mayor Maurice Tobin of that city had persuaded the Navy to lend Ted to him and the annual game that supported the mayor's charity benefiting poor children. The event would include an exhibition game between players in the military and the Boston Braves and a home-run hitting contest between Ted and Babe Ruth. The latter had begun his career as a pitcher with the Red Sox in 1915 and retired as a Brave in 1935. The paths of the Kid and the 48-year-old Sultan of Swat had never crossed paths, until July 12, 1943.

When Ruth met Ted, he blared, "Hiya, kid," while pumping the star-struck young man's hand. "You remind me a lot of myself. I love to hit. You're one of the most natural ballplayers I've ever seen. And if my record is broken, I hope you're the one to do it."

Dick Flavin, the longtime public address announcer and poet laureate of the Red Sox, provided me with the following account:

Williams was brought up from preflight school in North Carolina for what should be considered one of the most famous days in baseball. Ruth was recruited to manage the all-stars. The Braves were the home team but because Red Sox owner Tom Yawkey had offered its use, the event was held at Fenway Park. Ted, for the only time there, wore a road team gray Boston uniform. Ruth, because he always traveled with it, wore a Yankees home uniform.

Williams arrived at the park wearing his Navy uniform, and was introduced to Ruth. The newspapers of the day described him as being "tongue tied," a condition not normally associated with the outspoken slugger. Asked about it years later, Ted confirmed the description. "I was flabbergasted," he said. "He was Babe Ruth, for God's sake!" The event took place on the Monday before the All-Star game, played in Philadelphia that year, which might explain why it is not more famous. All the baseball beat writers and big-time columnists were in the City of Brotherly Love for the big game. The local newspapers covered the Boston event but didn't play it up very much. Ted was only twenty-four and, though he'd already hit .406, hadn't achieved the iconic status of his later years. Ruth was nine years retired from baseball but still relatively young. It was assumed that there would be many more meetings between the two. But, by the time Ted was discharged from the service and back with the Red Sox, Babe was already sick with the cancer from which he would die in 1948.

When he appeared on the field Williams was given a lusty cheer, but it was dwarfed by the reception accorded to Ruth. In pregame ceremonies Babe took the microphone and his showman's instincts won over the crowd. "Boston's my starting town," he said. "Here's the town I love." If there ever was a Curse of the Bambino it was unbeknownst to Babe Ruth.

Then the home-run competition began. Each player was allotted ten swings. Ted, who hadn't faced big league pitching in almost ten months, deposited three home-run balls into the seats. Then came the Babe. On his second swing he fouled the ball off his ankle and yowled in pain. He hobbled around for a few more swings, but the ankle swelled up and he sat down without hitting one ball hard.

In the seventh inning of the game, with the all-stars trailing, Ted hit a game-winning homer ten rows deep into the centerfield bleachers. That got Ruth's competitive juices flowing and in the eighth inning he inserted himself as a pinch hitter. The result was what the newspapers described as a fly ball to short right field. It must have been pretty short right field because the putout was made by Tony Cuccinello, the second baseman. It had begun as the Babe's day, but it ended with a virtuoso performance by Teddy.[1]

---

[1] The two great hitters would actually compete one more time. On July 28, an exhibition game was played at Yankee Stadium between the Chapel Hill Cloudbusters and the Yanklands, a team of players from the Yankees and Indians managed by Babe Ruth. The Hall of Famer was a pinch-hitter in the sixth inning. He managed a long foul to right, then walked. This would be the Babe's final appearance as a player in a major league stadium. He died five years later at only 53.

Then it was back to focusing on preparing to fly in combat. Ted and Pesky were assigned to the Bunker Hill Naval Air Station in Kokomo, Indiana. Upon arrival, Ted recalled in *My Turn at Bat*, he looked up and the "air was black with planes." There were 150 of them circling above with nothing but "a big round mat that everybody's landing on. It looked like flies on a garbage can." Difficulties flying—Ted recalled that Pesky "flew an airplane like he had stone arms"—and especially landing at the Kokomo base was what washed Pesky out of aviation: "Poor John lines up the runway, comes in and, *whoosh*, the wind blows him away." According to Ted, this cycle continued, with Pesky making eight total approaches in the same day. The little shortstop stayed in the Navy and eventually became an officer, but he stayed out of the cockpit. Pesky, whom Ted always called "Needle" because of his long, narrow nose, would not be reunited with his good friend until after the war.

Next stop for Ted was Pensacola, in December. There, Ted cared as much (or more!) about his introduction to Florida fishing as he did about being a pilot. As was his way, he soon excelled at both . . . with one exception. During one practice run, Ted blacked out at 17,000 feet, and his plane went into a dive. With only 2,000 feet left before crashing, he regained consciousness. Instead of panicking, Ted took control of the aircraft, and its underside scraped treetops as he pulled it out of the dive.

Another Christmas, another stay at the base for Ted. This time, at least, he received a package of brownies that Doris's grandmother had baked for him. According to Bill Nowlin's book, Ted had a routine day, which meant that if he had some free time, he could reply to his fan mail. Ted tried to respond to every letter, with the ones from children on the top of the pile.

Other than that frightening incident at 17,000 feet, he did so well at flying that the Navy made him an instructor. On May 2, 1944, he was commissioned as a Marine Corps second lieutenant. Being an instructor did not mean Ted was going to sit out the war. In fact, he put in for duty in the Pacific, and he was sent across the state to

Jacksonville for combat training (where, of course, like batting .400, he set a new student gunnery record). That 20-20 (or better) vision didn't hurt! Later, the enemy would learn that Williams could see them long before they could spot his plane, a life-saving advantage.

Finally, he received his deployment orders. But the Japanese couldn't hold out long enough to take on Ted Williams. He was in San Francisco in August 1945, right after qualifying for landings on an aircraft carrier, waiting to ship out, when the war ended. He had been assigned to a base in Hawaii, but on December 4, a troop ship that included Ted arrived in San Diego. Both his mother and Doris were there to welcome him home.

***

Someone wishing to go into broadcasting today has a wide range of options—not just podcasts, streaming, and other Internet outlets in addition to radio and television, but hundreds (if not more) of programs at colleges and universities, many of them with well-equipped studios. One can even go for graduate degrees in the field and pay hundreds of dollars for textbooks along the way. My graduate school was WSAM, Big SAM Radio in Saginaw, Michigan, a short distance from the shore of Lake Huron. Salary: $2 an hour. Education: Priceless.

I expanded on the in-the-trenches knowledge I'd acquired while broadcasting during my college years, and having grown up on a farm, I already knew there was no substitute for hard work. There was no regular sports show at WSAM, but I did pretty much everything else—morning disc jockey, afternoon DJ, evening DJ, newsman, weekends, and sitting in for anyone out sick or on vacation. I sure heard our regular playlist of Frank Sinatra, Bing Crosby, Rosemary Clooney, Nat King Cole, big bands, and show tunes enough times. A big bonus was that Big SAM carried Tigers broadcasts, so during the games I was actually getting paid just to listen to Van Patrick's radio call, with my only role being to break in every half-hour for the

mandatory station identification. ("You're listening to Tigers baseball on WSAM, Big Sam in Saginaw.")

I hadn't expected it, but after I graduated Central Michigan, several professors urged me to further my education by earning a Master's Degree in health science. I applied to a number of schools, and
when Indiana University accepted me with the offer of an annual
$1,000 stipend as a graduate assistant, the decision was made. I could
keep my job at WSAM during the summers. This was great because
I had come to be keenly interested in broadcasting, and I wasn't
being forced (yet) to choose between it and becoming a teacher and
coach. On a warm September day in 1957—aware that my hero, Ted
Williams, now 39, was leading all of baseball in batting—I climbed
into my bulky, seven-year-old Chrysler Imperial and drove south to
Bloomington.

As luck would have it, Indiana University had just hired Richard
Yoakum, the news director at KCRG Radio in Cedar Rapids, Iowa,
to be a professor of broadcast journalism. He was a 33-year-old pipe-
smoking dynamo who didn't let having suffered from polio as a child
stop him from being highly mobile on crutches, as well as anyone,
and play golf, too. An immediate goal of his was to establish WFIU,
the campus FM radio station, as the broadcaster of Indiana University football and basketball games in the Big Ten. I was one of fifteen
students who showed up at a football scrimmage to audition as a
play-by-play announcer. Soon after, Yoakum informed me that I
had the job. My partner as color commentator would be Phil Jones,
a junior. This would turn out to be an auspicious beginning for the
university's sports coverage, as Phil went on to spend 32 years with
CBS News, including working as a war correspondent in Vietnam
and a White House television beat reporter. The Enberg-Jones team
became the very first voices of the Indiana University sports network.
Who knew?

Although the late 1950s were lean times for Hoosier football, I
was having a blast. During my first broadcast back home at historic
Michigan Stadium, when Indiana took on the Wolverines, in the

booth next door was Tom Harmon, "Old 98." Tom had grown up in Indiana, won the Heisman Trophy at the University of Michigan in 1940, and three years earlier had been inducted into the College Football Hall of Fame. (And like Ted Williams, he was a pilot during World War II, actually seeing combat in the Pacific Theater.) Here I was at 22 next door to a legend, and making $35 a game. Oh my!

In case you're wondering, during this time at IU, I first used the expression "Oh my!" Indiana basketball was very successful then. The team was nicknamed the "Hurryin' Hoosiers" because the coach, Branch McCracken, passionately favored the fast break. Pass first, dribble only if you had to, then shoot the ball. One night, when the Hoosiers were on an up-tempo roll, it just came out of my mouth in one long burst: "OOOOOHHHHH MY!!!" Everyone listening to the broadcast heard it. That week, campus friends greeted me with, "Hi, Dick . . . Oh my!" It's been a good friend ever since, that exclamation point, alerting the audience that something exciting has happened—it's universal, whether at Wimbledon, baseball games, football contests, the Olympics, or all the other events I've covered. My mother must have been proud because she used it frequently, too, often in dismay at my behavior: "Oh my, Richard, wait til your father gets home."

After just one year, I had a Master's Degree. But except for heading up to Saginaw for the summer, I remained at Indiana University, as a graduate instructor on campus, studying for a doctorate, and importantly, this also allowed me to continue to broadcast games on the expanding WFIU sports network . . . and to meet my first wife.

After the newlyweds settled into on-campus married housing, I pursued becoming Dr. Enberg. Working toward a doctorate did not interfere with broadcasting duties, as I continued the play-by-play of IU football and basketball. I even got a raise . . . from $35 to $50. It was a lot of work, but not that that had stopped me before.

As I was applying the finishing edits on my doctoral dissertation in the spring of 1961, right after the IU basketball season ended, a Columbus, Ohio, television station asked if I would be interested in calling the play-by-play of Ohio State's NCAA basketball regional game in Louisville, Kentucky. Unlike today's March Madness saturation of the air waves, at that time there was no national telecast of the NCAA Tournament, not even the championship game. I accepted in a heartbeat and hung on for the ride. The Ohio State Buckeyes were the defending national champions and featured Jerry Lucas, John Havlicek, Mel Nowell, and a role player named Bobby Knight. They had nearly gone unbeaten in the 1960-61 season, 27-1 overall, losing only to (in a game I called) Indiana University and Walt Bellamy in Bloomington. The Columbus station liked my work and offered me the chance to call the finals in Kansas City.

Ohio State had defeated Kentucky in the regional final and then, in the Final Four in Kansas City, routed St. Joseph's to take a long winning streak into the national championship game against second-ranked Cincinnati. I had never flown before. A TWA Constellation delivered me safely for what would be the only telecast of the game in the entire country. During the consolation game between St. Joseph's and Utah, I dutifully studied my championship game notes. I was flying solo, with no color analyst.

Then a problem, a *big* problem, occurred. The "national" telecast, although going only to Columbus and Cincinnati (we've come a long way!), was due to go on the air at 9 p.m. EST. But the consolation game between Utah and St. Joseph's for third place had labored into overtime. If they finished that game in the first overtime, we'd be okay. But when 9 o'clock hit, they were still playing. It took four overtimes for St. Joseph's to emerge victorious. Not expecting any involvement in that game, I had not prepared a single decent thought. I scrambled desperately to get lineups, any information at all. I've never called a game with so little preparation. Suddenly, what was supposed to be a pretty easy, well-rehearsed five-minute lead-in to the championship game had become a nightmarish "throw Enberg in the fire" test.

On the fly, I managed to pick up names of players and somewhat professionally faked and hopefully fooled the audience through the four overtimes. But the challenge was hardly over. Now I had to fill the requisite 30-minute hiatus while Ohio State and Cincinnati took the court to warm up. I dashed around the arena grabbing people for interviews, and I think the only person left was the guy sweeping the floor. He would have been next. But this was a very good break for me. In a terrific contest, Cincinnati dramatically upset Ohio State 70-65 . . . in overtime. And I had somehow survived.

Then it was back to Indiana writing and teaching. It still hadn't occurred to me that broadcasting was my future. When San Fernando Valley State College offered me positions as a teacher of health education and assistant baseball coach, with a wife and newly minted doctorate in tow, it was time to return to California.

***

By the time Ted arrived in San Diego, soon to be officially discharged from the Marine Corps, he had turned 27. (He chose to remain in the Marine Corps Reserves with a promotion to captain, a decision that would have big consequences a few years later.) He had missed three full years of major league baseball, from ages 25 to 27. He wasn't the only star to make such a sacrifice: it was the same for Joe and Dominic DiMaggio, Hank Greenberg, Johnny Pesky, and others, and even longer for Bob Feller, who did see action in the Pacific Theater, much of it aboard the USS Alabama, earning eight battle stars. (An injury to Rapid Robert's right hand almost ended his career, but an operation performed by a ship's surgeon, Wilson Scanlon, successfully repaired the damage and helped propel Feller on to the Hall of Fame.)

Ted had played baseball during his three-year absence from MLB, such as his experiences with the Cloudbusters while he was in Chapel Hill. Still, these weren't real games. Ted, along with other ball players who had served in the branches of America's armed forces, had to wonder if he could be a major league player again. More than that, in the 1946 season, could he return to the Triple Crown level of excellence he had achieved when he left Boston in 1942? Or ever?

When Ted headed back to Boston in 1946, he had a wife in tow. He and Doris Soule might have been married for several years by then, had it not been for Navy regulations: "If a cadet marries before being commissioned he would be breaking his induction oath. The applicant must be unmarried, must never have been married, and must not marry—openly or secretly—until he gets his wings." Doris dutifully waited until Ted was commissioned, and they had finally married on May 4, 1944. During the winter before heading east, Ted and Doris had lived with May Williams.

Trying to make up in a few weeks for three years of next to no hitting, Ted bloodied his hands beating ball after ball, using a heavier than usual bat. However much natural talent he possessed, Ted believed the key to baseball success was outworking the other guy. Overjoyed to have traded in his military uniform for his baseball flannels, he was enthusiastic about Boston's prospects and unusually open to reporters—although when a *Time* magazine writer asked him about this, Ted responded, "I'm always nice enough in the spring, until I read what those shitheads write about me." Usually, for public consumption, his sarcastic term for reporters was "Knights of the Keyboard."

Another word about Ted's relationship with the Boston press. It is true that he had "rabbit ears," more aware than most athletes of what the fans in the stands offered and what the writers reported, especially if it was negative. The Boston press in the 1940s and '50s was notorious for its harshness, and Ted gave it right back to them. His retaliation, though, was exactly what the writers wanted. One journalist in particular, Dave Egan, a columnist for the *Boston Record*, took a special dislike to Ted, probably because the brash slugger wouldn't kiss his ring.

As Halberstam described Egan in his wonderful book *Summer of '49*, "Gentle and kind when sober, he became, when drinking, a monster, a man with the foulest tongue imaginable. . . . What he did, especially to Williams, was not pleasant for anyone who cares about the American press. His coverage amounted to a vendetta." (The legendary college coach Bobby Knight—who also had a touchy relationship with the press—recently reminded me that he would be asked by reporters how he could possibly be good friends with Ted Williams. Bobby always replied, "I like HIM because he doesn't like YOU.")

While the toxic Colonel Egan and other Boston writers relished the opportunity to attack Ted for his bad manners and combative attitude, the fans, young and old, cheered and adored the hitting genius. One of those was a young schoolboy from South Boston, Ray Flynn, who idolized Teddy Ballgame. In 1947, Flynn, age 10, was selling newspapers at Fenway Park. The *Boston American* sold for 3 cents a paper. His quota was 75 per day. He told me that most fans would pay him a nickel, and he mastered the art of fumbling for change until the buyer would relent and let him keep the change, his tip. He confirmed that when the papers arrived, he would first search the sports pages and read Egan's column. If the Colonel ripped Ted, Flynn would rip as well, tearing out that page of all 75 papers. Many years later, Ray Flynn would become Mayor of the City of Boston.

According to the more objective (and sober) members of the press, the Boston Red Sox on paper looked to be the team to beat. Joe Cronin was now the full-time manager, having played his last game the previous April and retired with a career .301 average. The core group of Ted, Dom DiMaggio, Johnny Pesky, and Bobby Doerr (who had also served in the military) was joined by Rudy York, obtained from the Tigers, and Wally Moses (during the season) from the White Sox. (In 1942, Jimmie Foxx had been dealt to the Chicago Cubs, and he finished his career in 1945 with the Philadelphia Athletics.) A strong starting rotation—Tex Hughson, Boo Ferriss, Mickey Harris, and Joe Dobson—also made a big difference for Boston.

They turned out to be the team to beat on the field, too. After just two months, and even with Joe DiMaggio back with the Yankees, the Red Sox had a 41-9 record and a 1-game lead over New York. The other teams in the American League were stunned, and sometimes desperate measures were employed. The most well known was the Lou Boudreau experiment.

In the first game of a June doubleheader, Ted tore apart the Cleveland Indians with three home runs, one a grand slam and the third in the bottom of the ninth, for an 11-10 triumph. Boudreau, both the shortstop and manager of the Indians, was especially frustrated by having a homer and four doubles yet no victory. In the second game, after Ted had doubled in three runs in the first inning, when he next came up to the plate he observed that only the left fielder was to the left of second base—there were six players on the right side of the infield and outfield. Initially, the shift seemed effective because the rest of the game, Ted grounded to second and walked twice. But by the end of the season, he batted .400 against Cleveland with nine home runs—the shift means nothing when a ball lands in the seats. But there would be a time when the shift would haunt him.

He continued to enjoy the season as the Red Sox were running on all cylinders. And there was the All-Star Game that July, with that "eephus pitch" home run that so enthralled this impressionable youngster. Somewhat lost in all the attention that one at-bat received was that in the game Ted went 4-for-4 and became the first player to drive in five runs in an All-Star Game.

Attendance at Fenway Park and throughout the major leagues was up as the postwar population flocked to the ballparks, grateful the diluted version of baseball was over. When the season ended, an all-time high of 18.5 million people had passed through the turnstiles. More people than ever were seeing the greatest stars in baseball and, in Ted's case, a player reaching his peak.

During the dog days of summer, it seemed that all Ted and his teammates had to do was keep breathing and the American League pennant was theirs. Suddenly, the Sox fell into a hitting slump. The Tigers, once behind by 16 games, began creeping up. The Boston traveling secretary had bought cases of champagne for the clinching celebration, and for two weeks they had to be hauled from city to city. The Kid was as guilty as anyone for the team's downturn, hitting only .250 in September.

Finally, though, on September 13, Ted hit his only inside-the-park homer—against the Indians, driving the ball over the left fielder's head—and Hughson's 1-0 shutout gave the title to the Red Sox.

Nevertheless, Ted's slump had cost him the batting title, which went to Mickey Vernon, a rare bright spot for the Washington Senators. In his last great year, Hank Greenberg of the Tigers earned the home run and RBI titles. (It should be noted that when Greenberg returned from military service, he was a grizzled 34. I wonder what numbers he would have registered during those three war years by a guy who in his 13 seasons *averaged* 38 homers and 148 RBIs.) Meanwhile, Ted delivered a .342 season with 38 homers and 123 RBIs, earning his second MVP Award. With the Red Sox winning the pennant by 12 games and boasting a 104-50 record, the writers couldn't rob him this time.

Boston's World Series opponent would be the St. Louis Cardinals, led by Stan Musial and his .365 batting average, Red Schoendienst, and Enos Slaughter. The Cards' dramatic season had ended in a playoff game with the Brooklyn Dodgers. Meanwhile, the Boston players, with two weeks of meaningless games to finish up the season, had been twiddling their thumbs. A costly decision was made that the Red Sox, to refresh their skills, would play a tune-up game before the World Series began. It took place on a cold day in Boston against an ad hoc all-star team. During it, Ted was hit by a pitch, on the elbow, which turned blue. So there was that physical problem, then a bit of a mental one when "Colonel" Dave Egan, back on the hate-Ted bandwagon, reported that as soon as the World Series was over, he would be traded to Detroit.

You wouldn't think that hero worship would have any place between adversaries in the World Series, but it seems especially with Ted Williams, it was hard to resist. In his biography, Ben Bradlee Jr. includes this priceless anecdote from the Redbirds' young catcher, Joe Garagiola. He was all of 20 in the 1946 Fall Classic and had grown up in St. Louis listening on the radio to Browns baseball games against other American League teams. No one tormented the Browns more than Ted did, and Garagiola was in awe of him. Suddenly, in that first game, when Ted dug in for his first at-bat: "There he was right in front of me. I didn't know whether to throw the ball to the pitcher or ask for an autograph. The first pitch was an inside fastball, and he followed it all the way into my mitt. 'That ball was inside,' he said to me. 'Yes, sir,' I said to him, and that was all I could say."

It turned into a seesaw World Series. In St. Louis, Rudy York's home run won the first Series game for Boston, 3-2. In the second game, the Red Sox faced the left-hander Harry Brecheen. The 31-year-old had gone only 15-15 during the season, but in the Series he gave the kind of performance that would be recalled in future Fall Classics when discussing Mickey Lolich of the Tigers and Madison Bumgardner of the San Francisco Giants. Brecheen won the second and the sixth games. And he would pitch in the seventh game, too. In that second game, Brecheen tossed a 3-0 shutout and Ted went hitless. (Ted compared Brecheen to the Yankees' Ed Lopat, both lefties who threw a lot of off-speed pitches—"junk," in Ted's terms.)

In Boston, the Red Sox bounced back behind Boo Ferriss and his 4-0 blanking of the Cards. Another highlight was York's three-run homer and Ted, with two outs and the wind blowing in from right, bunting toward third base for a single. A victory in Game Four would send the Sox into their third home game with a 3-1 lead in the Series. Instead, their pitching fell apart and the Cardinals strolled to a 12-2 win. Now the pressure was on Boston not to head west in a 3-2 hole. They responded with Ted singling and driving in a run in the first inning, the Sox scoring six runs in the game, and Joe Dobson making the lead last for a 6-3 win. They went to St. Louis needing just one win for the first Red Sox championship since 1918.

However, by then, Ted had managed only four hits and one run batted in. Given that, Boston's lead in the Series was especially impressive. Apparently unimpressed was Brecheen, whose nickname was "the Cat." The Sox could scratch out only one run against the little lefty, on a Bobby Doerr sacrifice fly, and lost 4-1. In the seventh game, Ferriss would be sent out against the righthander Murry Dickson, who had been 15-6 on the season. This game, on a warm and sunny day in St. Louis, would have one of the most famous finishes in World Series history.

The game was on October 14. Ferriss pitched a strong game but got nicked for three runs early. Dominic DiMaggio drove in the only Red Sox run, and going into the eighth inning, Boston was down 3-1. Pinch-hit singles by Rip Russell and Catfish Metkovich began the top of the inning. They were still on base when DiMaggio came up, but now there were two outs after Wally Moses had fanned and Johnny Pesky had lined out to center fielder Enos Slaughter. DiMaggio took a strike, then Brecheen, in relief just one day after his complete-game victory, missed on the next three tosses. The 3-1 pitch was on the outside part of the plate, and DiMaggio drove it to right-center. It banged off the wall, and while Slaughter chased it, Russell and Metkovich scored easily, tying the game at 3-3. Slaughter later confided that if DiMaggio's double had been another foot and a half toward center field, it would have landed in the seats because there was no screen in center. That would have given the Red Sox a 4-3 lead. The close call gained significance because the next man up was Ted, and Brecheen induced a pop-up, leaving the score knotted.

Also very significant: DiMaggio sprinting from first to second on his double had heard his hamstring pop. He staggered to second and called for time. Joe Cronin, who had been coaching third in addition to managing, rushed to his center fielder, who could barely walk, let alone run. He would have to be replaced by Leon Culberson. Dom DiMaggio, who David Halberstam stated was "arguably the most aggressive centerfielder of his era," would not be on the field when the Cardinals came to bat.

This would prove to be the pivotal event of the entire Series. After just missing the home run, DiMaggio was out of the game. The Red Sox not only had narrowly missed gaining the lead, but now they had lost their best outfielder, a double dose of bad luck. Culberson was less talented defensively and threw left-handed, a factor that would critically come to play in the next inning.

In the bottom of the eighth, with two outs, Slaughter danced off first and Harry Walker came to the plate. From the dugout, DiMaggio was signaling Culberson, trying to get him to take a few steps closer to Ted in left. However, he didn't, and sure enough Walker hit his patented line drive over the shortstop's head, the ball aiming right between Ted and Culberson.

"Culberson has to backtrack to make sure the ball doesn't get by the two of them so he backtracks," Dominic recalled in his memoir about the 1941 season. "I would never have had to backtrack. I would have been over enough that I would have made a right-angle turn and cut the ball off. And I said all along that I would have had a shot at Slaughter at third base. I'd already thrown three guys out in that series and they had stopped running."

But Slaughter never stopped running. In what became known as his "Mad Dash," he simply kept his legs pumping around second and third, daring the Red Sox to execute the relay perfectly. They didn't. Not expecting Slaughter to keep running, Culberson made a routine toss to Pesky, the cutoff man. His first look was to second to make sure Walker wasn't trying to stretch the single. It was only then he spotted Slaughter heading for home—either no teammate had yelled out what was happening, or he couldn't hear it above the sound of the Cardinals crowd. Pesky's desperate throw was offline, and Slaughter scored. Slaughter said afterward, "If they hadn't taken DiMaggio out of the game, I wouldn't have tried it." All Ted could do was watch helplessly as the Boston tragedy unfolded.

The lead held up. The Cardinals won the game and the World Series 4-3. That Ted performed so poorly in the Fall Classic was, yes, a big deal at the time but over time became much bigger. One reason was that during his career he rose to the occasion many times, especially with dramatic home runs, shouldering the majority of Boston's offensive production season after season. But the 1946 Series was also magnified years later when it turned out that Ted would not play in one again. Ty Cobb, with the astonishing .366 career average, batted just .200 in his first World Series, then hit .368 in his next one. (In two World Series, Honus Wagner managed only .228 and .240.) In his first Fall Classic, Musial batted .222, but he was able to play in three more. Babe Ruth's first postseason experience was a dismal one at .118, but he would have six more chances to improve. Not Ted.

Basically, Ted Williams had just the one shot, and he didn't deliver. And no one was more aware of that than he was. Rather than hide or make excuses, for the rest of his life Ted blamed himself for the Red Sox not being world champions that year. A half-century later, Ted was asked what was the one thing out of a very active, full life he would have done differently. He responded, "I'd have done better in the '46 World Series. God, I would."

The fact that my hero was being chastised in the press for having a bad World Series on the game's biggest stage made him all the more human to me. He wasn't perfect—only damn close. From my radio seat on the Michigan farm I felt badly but predicted boldly that he would be back and make all the critics eat their words. Perhaps with some subconscious solidarity, the first rock that I hit that weekend, I fouled off.

On that dismal, mid-October day in 1946, perhaps finally paying back that $20 loan from 1938 or just too disgusted with himself, Ted would give his World Series check to Johnny Orlando, who later confided that in the St. Louis clubhouse shower, Ted "cried like a baby."

"Sick inside," after the Fenway Park clubhouse had cleared out, Ted showered and changed, then made his way to the hotel. He packed, preparing to leave Boston right away. After arriving at the station, Ted climbed into his train compartment and started to cry—with several people bearing witness.

No doubt Ted was embarrassed by this display of great emotion, but it is good for people to be reminded that heroes shed tears, too. They too care.

***

At the future Cal State Northridge (then still San Fernando Valley State), I was dedicated to being a college professor. And I taught there for four years. During this time, my first and second children were born, Jennifer and Andrew. Sure, I couldn't forget broadcasting after years spent doing Big Ten football and basketball and pieces of just about everything else. But I was now devoted to teaching and being a dad.

Nevertheless, on an annual professor's salary of less than $5,000, a side job would be a good idea, in fact, a necessary one. I took my tapes from Indiana and contacted virtually every radio and TV station in the Los Angeles market, and followed up with phone calls. Only when I thought to introduce myself as "Dr. Enberg" did secretaries think I was a physician and arrange interview appointments. It wasn't in sports, but I did get a part-time job, as a disc jockey at KGIL Radio in the San Fernando Valley. I enjoyed the paycheck but still didn't view it as being on my way into broadcasting, only a means to supplement a poor professor's income.

However, in 1963, I took another radio job, this one with KNX, a CBS affiliate, doing sports reports on the weekends. There I met two broadcasting veterans, Chuck Benedict and Pat McGuirk, who saw some reasonable potential in me in the business. Benedict helped me get a second substitute job at KLAC Radio doing weekend sports reports. That in turn led me to covering a USC-UCLA match . . . well, not football, but water polo. (I jokingly have said I don't know how they got the horses in the pool.) I took the job, never having even seen a water polo match. However, there I was broadcasting one with Olympic swimmer Roy Saari on Channel 11. And that led to me being hired by the TV station to do play-by-play of LA State's 1964 football season. More good luck: they went 9-0 and ended the season as the nation's top-ranked small college team. The dots were connecting.

Something else happened in 1964 that would have a major impact. By then, the great cowboy movie and singing star Gene Autry owned not only the expansion Los Angeles Angels baseball club and KMPC Radio, but added KTLA (Channel 5) to his holdings. He hired Bob

Speck as sports director, whose mandate was to develop all the sports programming we could gather. KTLA had been experimenting with a rotation of active athletes—including Jerry West and Rudy LaRusso of the Lakers, Roosevelt Grier of the Rams, Jim Fregosi of the Angels, and my future broadcast partners Merlin Olsen of the Rams and Don Drysdale of the Dodgers—as sports reporters on the nightly news. Speck began looking for one person to be the regular sports segment reporter. I auditioned.

I was given the job, with a 13-week trial period. San Fernando Valley State gave me a leave of absence, which would allow me to return to education in case I fell on my broadcasting face. I never taught there again because in the next 18 months, I was not only the KTLA sports anchor, but I was broadcasting weekly boxing from the Olympic Auditorium, UCLA basketball, and Angels pre- and postgame shows on TV, and the Rams on the radio. It was almost like hitting a home run in the All-Star Game. Oh my!

Part IV
The Best Years of His Life

Understandably, the bitter disappointment of losing the 1946 World Series in the last inning of the seventh game could have ushered in years of lackluster Red Sox teams. Instead, the seasons that followed were several of the most exciting and somewhat successful ones in the club's history. Why? One reason is long before there was a lot of ballyhoo over the Yankees' "core four" of Derek Jeter, Mariano Rivera, Andy Pettitte, and Jorge Posada, there was the Red Sox core four of Ted Williams, Dominic DiMaggio, Bobby Doerr, and Johnny Pesky, who played at the peak of their abilities. The Boston Red Sox proved to be a resilient and durable team. Another reason was Ted wouldn't let the team fold their tents and slink away. He was an Olympian who could carry the club on his broad shoulders and powerful swing.

But . . . we're talking about the Red Sox, so there must be a third reason: for the Boston fans, the anguish of 1946 wasn't enough—there would be more where that came from.

The rest of the 1940s was the best of times and the worst of times for Ted. Best, because few pitchers could get him out. In the 1947-49 seasons, the *lowest* he hit was .343, and he twice achieved his career-high RBI totals. He would still be only 31 when the '49 season ended, so one would assume Ted would perform at that level well into the 1950s and along the way Boston would nab that world championship that eluded them in '46 . . . maybe even two or three, especially as Joe DiMaggio became older and more banged up and the Yankees would presumably fade. But while the war overseas had ended, the war that was a big part of Ted's playing life continued.

The Boston organization certainly didn't blame Ted for the end of the '46 season, with Tom Yawkey offering him a $70,000 contract. He couldn't wait for spring training and then for the season to begin, to offer him a chance to make up for the end of the previous season.

However, midway through May he was hitting only .220. Not only was Lou Boudreau up to his old tricks by employing a shift, but also other managers were trying variations of it. The other teams in the American League were ganging up on Ted, and opposing pitchers were all trying to force him to pull the ball. What would have been hits in the past often became groundball outs.

No need to feel sorry for Ted, though, whose combination of keen intelligence and preparation paid off in June as his hitting took off, and he even derived some satisfaction from doubling and singling in the 1947 All-Star Game off the previous October's nemesis, Harry Brecheen. Ted had spent a lot of time during spring training talking to Hall of Famer Paul "Big Poison" Waner (.333 career average), a left-handed batter with the Pittsburgh Pirates, about hitting to left field.

The year 1947 will always have extraordinary significance for major league baseball: Jackie Robinson broke the color barrier. Ted had encountered Jackie in 1936 when their high schools in Southern California had played each other, but as an American Leaguer, the only way Ted would cross paths with Jackie would be in the World Series, if the Red Sox and Brooklyn Dodgers got that far. In July, though, Larry Doby became the first black player in the American League, brought up by the Cleveland Indians. As Doby told author Ben Bradlee Jr., "[Ted] just gave me a feeling of being welcome, which was important to me, especially when you had a lot of other people not saying anything. Didn't have to make any big deal out of it. That's why I feel it was from the heart."

No matter how potent the Boston lineup was, pitching was a problem. After two years possessing a strong staff, the Red Sox had to try to overcome a familiar bugaboo in the '47 season—spotty starting pitching. Not only did Boo Ferriss, Tex Hughson, and Mickey Harris have arm ailments, but their careers pretty much ended. They went from a combined 62 victories in 1946 to a dismal 29. Joe Dobson had a strong year at 18-8, but most of the other arms Joe Cronin called upon managed only .500 records.

Before resuming with Ted and that '47 season, Boston fans especially might indulge a detour about a significant event that year in the history of what would ultimately become the Green Monster, which Ted, though not the best outfielder, handled well for 18 seasons. Again, my thanks to the Red Sox public address announcer Dick Flavin for allowing me to use the following:

For the first thirty-five years of Fenway Park, the left-field wall wasn't even green. No one knew what the color of the wall was. It was totally covered in advertisements, everything from shaving cream to cab companies to Old Demon Rum. It wasn't until 1947 that owner Tom Yawkey had the ads exorcised and the wall painted what was referred to as "Dartmouth green" that it was given its present color. Even then it wasn't the Green Monster.

As late as the 1960s, if the term "monster" was used around the ballpark it referred to Dick "The Monster" Radatz, the huge (six feet six inches and listed as two hundred thirty pounds but must have been at least fifty more) relief pitcher who intimidated opposing hitters with his size and blazing fastball. His size and strength made him seem absolutely indestructible, so Red Sox management of the day proceeded unknowingly to destroy him. In the four years between 1962 and 1965 he was used for an average of 134 innings a year (a closer today averages 70 to 80 innings annually). It wasn't uncommon to see Radatz come into a game in the fourth or fifth inning, close it out, and be called upon again the next day. Even the Monster couldn't keep going at that rate and he was traded away in 1966, his fastball long gone.

The Green Monster in those days was usually used to describe a long, challenging golf course. But gradually the term took hold as the name of choice for what we old timers still refer to as The Wall. And a pretty good name it is, too, because it has certainly caused its share of nightmares. In 1912, when people got their first look at the left-field wall, they thought it was an imposing structure but nobody thought it possible to hit a ball over it (it was the dead ball era, remember). Very few even thought anyone would ever hit a ball against it. But in the first inning of just the fifth regular season game of the 1912 season, backup first baseman Hugh Bradley lashed a drive against it for a double, the first time it had ever been hit. Fans in the stands were still talking about it when, in the seventh, Bradley came up again and actually hit a game-winning home run over the wall and out onto Landsdown Street. I am certain that Bradley, a Holy Cross alum, couldn't forget that home run, especially since it's that last one he ever hit in the big leagues. He had a lifetime total of just two.

Once the wall was breached by Bradley's blow, others would follow and, with the arrival of the live ball era in 1920, they came early and often. The deluge has never stopped, although the Green Monster has probably taken away as many homers as it's given up. Many a screaming line drive, labeled for four hundred feet or more, has crashed off the top of the wall resulting in just a loud single. And countless lazy fly balls, routine outs in virtually any other ballpark, have just made it over the top for home runs (Hello, Bucky Dent.) The Green Monster and its idiosyncrasies have undergone changes over the years. It began as a plain wooden fence atop a ten-foot embankment in 1912, was rebuilt into its present dimensions, 37 feet high, in 1934, with a sheet of tin covering the wood (resulting in a loud *clang* when it was hit), then rebuilt again with a hard plastic replacing the tin-covered wood. A net was added in 1936 to protect neighboring businesses. The net was replaced by the Green Monster seats in 2003. Through it all, the Green Monster or The Wall (take your pick) has been an object of fascination by fans and players alike for more than a century, and that's not about to change.

When the season was over, Ted had earned his second Triple Crown thanks to a .343 average, 32 home runs, and 114 RBIs. Soon after, he learned that he had once again been denied the MVP Award in favor of Joe DiMaggio by a 202-201 tally. Joe's line had been .315, 20, and 97. As he had done in 1941 and '42, when the award had gone to DiMaggio and Joe Gordon, Ted could have gracefully acknowledged that the MVP most often goes to the player on a pennant-winning club. But this time was different, and more personal.

One of the writers who voted that year didn't put Ted's name on the MVP ballot at all. This apparently delusional writer (Ted erroneously thought it was a member of the Boston press corps) did not think that Ted, the Triple Crown winner, was one of the top 10 players in the American League that year. Even a tenth-place vote would have given Ted two points and thus the MVP Award. The viciously venomous scribe wanted to stick it to the Kid, and in doing so, he ensured the 1947 vote would be the worst in league history. As you can imagine, the shameful vote deepened Ted's bitter feelings about the Boston press and baseball reporting in general.

After the letdown of not repeating as American League champions in 1947, Ted also found a few fans and the occasional columnist in Boston carping that he cared more for his stats than if the Red Sox won or not. Ted came to the ballpark every day to play hard and he was beloved by teammates (especially his enduring core four comrades), so this criticism stung.

In turn, his relationship with those Boston fans became a real roller-coaster ride. They cheered when Ted knocked in a couple of runs or sent one into the stands. But fueled by the sarcastic or outright negative reporters, led by "Colonel" Egan, they could be quick to boo and shout nasty, sometimes very crude comments. Years earlier, Ted had stopped tipping his cap to fickle fans who applauded him, and even during the Red Sox peak years in the mid-to-late-1940s, he wasn't going to reverse that self-imposed ban.

Even the 1947-48 off-season would land Ted in a vat of controversy. Ted and Doris, pregnant during the summer and fall, were living in a Boston apartment in Brighton, a blue-collar section of Boston. She did not care much for baseball, so when Ted was not at Fenway Park or on the road, they entertained themselves by going to the movies and listening to jazz recordings. When Doris went into labor and gave birth to their daughter, Ted was still on a snook-fishing trip in the Florida Everglades. The press raked him over the coals for appearing insensitive and indifferent to the birth of his first child.

(A side note: At that time in our history, many fathers weren't there for the birth of their children, the feeling being that there wasn't anything they could do to help the process. I'm the first child of Arnie and Belle Enberg. My dad wasn't in the Mt. Clemens hospital when I was born. It certainly didn't make him a bad guy or the subject of criticism in the surrounding community.)

As soon as he received the call, Ted flew to Boston. The reporters didn't want to hear that Doris had delivered their baby two weeks early. He had planned to be there. It sure didn't help when Ted declared, "The hell with them. They can't run my life." To other reporters he said, "To heck with public opinion. It's my baby, and my life." Worse than that—and here it is hard to excuse the Kid—after a few days in Boston with his wife and newly named Bobby-Jo, Ted left again to continue fishing.

***

Early in my professional broadcasting days, I didn't have to fight with the press or anyone else. However, a different kind of fighting—specifically boxing—gave a big boost to my career.

In 1965, after only a few months at KTLA, I was assigned to broadcast the fights being held every Thursday night at the Olympic Auditorium in Los Angeles. The weekly series began shortly after the "phantom punch" delivered in the first round by Muhammad Ali in Lewiston, Maine, that knocked out Sonny Liston. At the time, it had tarnished boxing, and now I expected to be the one kayoed. But the broadcasts were an immediate ratings hit. If I was going to keep doing them, I had to know what I was talking about.

With help from Aileen Eaton, who ran the Olympic—she promoted fights at the auditorium for more than 40 years—and the boxing matchmaker Mickey Davies, and repeat visits to the Main Street Gym downtown, I learned the sport. I also learned why Aileen was known as the "Dragon Lady." She was relentlessly tough and abrasive—and this was to people she (sort of) liked! Before long, I was set to quit. But Davies ran some interference for me and Aileen backed off. Soon, boxing became the number one regularly scheduled program on KTLA. This, of course, meant expanding exposure for the young and ambitious ringside blow-by-blow man. But it sure was a bloody business. Up close, a bout is like watching an accident. From a distance or watching on TV, you don't realize how ferocious the punches are, and I was often no more than three feet away. From there, you not only hear the punches, you hear the reaction to them and you see the crimson-tainted spray that flies off the fighters. After one of my early telecasts, I couldn't determine what had caused the spots on my sports coat until I realized that they were perspiration, spit, and blood. I even had a mouthpiece land in my lap. Still, I would announce boxing matches regularly for three years, then return to it from time to time, including the 1976 national telecast of the Muhammad Ali-Richard Dunn heavyweight title bout from Munich, Germany.

Thankfully, I was not confined to boxing. The same year that I began doing the Olympic Auditorium events, I wrote a letter to Dan Reeves, owner of the Los Angeles Rams. I suggested, somewhat arrogantly, that I replace the ailing Bob Kelley, who had been the team's play-by-play man since the franchise had been founded in Cleveland in 1937. The letter was passed around and there was some "Who does this guy think he is?" scoffing, but Chuck Benedict, a member of the team's PR staff, who had long been a true supporter of my potential, arranged a generous helping hand. He gave me four passes to the last game of the 1965 season at the LA Coliseum and set up a work table on the press box roof. I would call the game and record it as an audition. A couple of my professor friends were drafted (pro bono) to be a spotter and a statistician.

It was cold and windy that December afternoon as the Rams hosted the Baltimore Colts. And no one was listening to my broadcast but a flock of seagulls lurking on the horizon, ready to harvest the fan's leftovers. But I was fortunate and understandably excited to have the opportunity. Fate was on my side: Don Shula's Colts defeated the Rams 20-17 to force a tie for the NFL Western Conference title between Baltimore and the Green Bay Packers. Remarkably, the Colts won without injured quarterbacks Johnny Unitas and Gary Cuozzo. The running back Tom Matte was the emergency quarterback, wearing a list of plays taped to his left wrist. In my experience, this was the first game in which a NFL quarterback wore a wristband with a game plan, a common practice today.

Rams owner, Dan Reeves, was intrigued by the audition tape. But while I awaited a decision about the 1966 season, CBS-TV okayed my application to do regional network postgame scoreboard shows from Los Angeles. This farm boy from Armada was going to be on network television for the first time. Oh, oh my! Then wouldn't you know, KMPC Radio, which broadcast the Rams games, also a part of Gene Autry's expanding broadcast empire, offered me the Sunday chair next to play-by-play man Bob Kelley. I couldn't say yes fast enough. As tempting as national TV was, I would now be working a full NFL schedule and groomed to take over for Kelley. I would be learning from one of the best.

And then I wasn't. While calling the third preseason game in horrible weather in Minnesota—it rained so hard, you couldn't see the field, and it was as if a firehose had been aimed at the windows of the booth—the conditions put extra strain on Kelley's fragile heart. He was advised to leave the broadcast booth. Then only 10 days after that Minnesota game, Kelley suffered a heart attack. He never recovered and died, two days before the Rams season opener. Despite my NFL inexperience, I was elevated to the first chair, and Dave Niehaus, who later became an icon as the voice of the Seattle Mariners, took my chair, which was barely warm.

I was told the 1966 football season would be an audition. If I passed the test, the job was mine. If I didn't, at least the Rams gave me a fair chance. It turned out that I would go on to call their games for the next dozen years. Most of them were highly successful seasons—after seven losing records in seven years, the franchise had the wisdom to hire George Allen as the head coach. He immediately went 8-6 in 1966, and, overall, in his five years with the team, he posted a sterling 49-19-4.

This was an opportune time to be announcing the games, especially since this was a team of which the fans, based on recent records, had few expectations. Allen, in our weekly pregame interviews, also pointed out something about myself as a broadcaster. One day he said, "Dick, I can tell you're really serious about your business." I asked what gave him that impression. "Because every time you come into my office your shoes are shined. That tells me you care about how you appear. It indicates that you're taking your job seriously." Thank you, Shinola!

Allen was right, I did. Preparation and taking my job seriously was something I had in common with my baseball idol, Ted Williams. In spring training and during the season, he'd spend hour after hour in batting cages, sometimes raising blisters on the tough skin of his big hands, all for the four to five chances he would have at the plate. He never slacked coming to the ballpark in plenty of time to prepare for a game. During the games he didn't lean back and relax by the water cooler; he studied pitchers relentlessly, searching for an edge, a weakness, a pattern to exploit. Even in the outfield, he practiced his stance and swing, a habit that drove a few of his managers nuts. When he got home after a game, he and Doris ate right away and he'd hit the sack not long after Bobby-Jo. It never occurred to Ted to go out on the town—he had another game the next day, and he had to be up early to prepare and feel his best. In addition to his enormous talent, Ted Williams was a baseball professional.

Me, I shined my shoes . . . and a whole lot more. With every passing year, I was feeling more like a broadcasting professional. Preparation has always been a major foundation for my broadcasting success. It was my version of always being ready to hit. I wanted to know more about players' and coaches' backgrounds than anyone else. It allowed me to personalize the athlete, to present him (or her) as much more than a number on a jersey. In one instance, a big defensive lineman was more than #74, he was a Utah farmer bailing and hauling hay in the summer and earning Academic All-American honors at Utah State during the school year. He also had a fondness for acting. He was Merlin Olsen, who became my immensely talented and beloved broadcast partner.

Merlin's story was like so many others, personal and inspiring. My own mother would embrace these stories—after describing a player who helped raise his younger siblings upon his mother's death, all the while practicing football and the cello, she related about how she cared about that player and would always root for him. The personal nuggets thus became "Mother's Notes." If she was touched, others would be, too.

***

When spring rolled around, a big change for the Red Sox in 1948 was that for the first time in many years, the team had a new manager. Joe Cronin had moved upstairs to general manager, and in something of a head-spinning move, longtime Yankees manager Joe McCarthy became the Boston skipper. Many Beantown reporters expected trouble between McCarthy, who stressed discipline and rules for the players, and the more freewheeling and spontaneous (and informal dresser) Ted. But right away, any possible conflict was avoided. When

McCarthy was asked about managing Ted, he replied, "If I can't get along with a .400 hitter, it'll be *my* fault." Ted wasn't as chummy with McCarthy as he had been with Cronin, but the two got along fine.

After all, Ted had more responsibilities than he had in the past. Number one on that list (aside from Doris and Bobby-Jo) was to earn Boston's second pennant in three seasons. Cronin in his new role spent the off-season rebuilding the starting rotation, and Dobson was joined by Ellis Kinder, Mel Parnell, and Jack Kramer. The biggest upgrade to the lineup was bringing shortstop Vern Stephens over from the St. Louis Browns. He replaced a fading Rudy York in the lineup.

This looked like wasted energy by the end of May, when the Red Sox were 11 games out of first place. McCarthy was irritated, but he was a veteran campaigner, and he wasn't about to get down on his team, at least not this early. The only player who seemed to have noticed that the season had started was Ted, who was batting a lusty .374. And as far as friction with his left-fielder, when Ted came back into the dugout after really ripping the ball, the skipper would stare straight ahead but make sure Ted heard, "If I could hit like you I'd play for nothing. I'd play this game for nothing." Ted relished this sort of comment from a man who had managed Lou Gehrig, Joe DiMaggio, Tommy Henrich, and other Yankees greats.

As the weather warmed, the Kid and his teammates became the comeback kids, clawing their way up the standings and fending off challenges from the Yankees (now managed by Bucky Harris) and Boudreau's Indians. The player-manager was having what would turn out to be an MVP season. With three weeks to play, the Red Sox had vaulted into first with a five-game lead over Cleveland. Then the Indians surged ahead while the Red Sox slumped, then they rallied again. To force a playoff, Boston had to win their last three games and hope the Tigers could take at least one game from Cleveland. In those three games, Ted had six hits, including two doubles in the final-game victory over the Yankees, who with an injury-plagued Joe DiMaggio had already been eliminated. On the last day of the 1948 season, with the Boston victory following the Tigers having beaten Cleveland, a one-game playoff was set for Fenway Park.

An amusing yet telling sidebar is that if the Red Sox beat the Indians to get to the World Series, would they have Dominic DiMaggio in his usual leadoff spot? The "Little Professor" had not shown much faith in his team—after all, he and his fiancée, Emily, had scheduled their wedding date for October 7. The conflict would be that if Boston won the pennant, that ceremony and getaway to the DiMaggios' honeymoon would be smack in the middle of the Fall Classic. During that last week of the season, Joe DiMaggio had called his mother. When Rosalie DiMaggio mentioned the wedding date and what would Dominic do, Joe told her, "I'll see that Dom is free to get married on the seventh."

And Joe tried his best. In those last two games of the season against Boston, a struggling Joe reached base 8 out of ten at-bats, but the Red Sox still prevailed. In the first game, a clutch-hitting Ted began the scoring with his 25th home run, and in the second game he led the way to a 10-5 win. Bring on the Indians.

The Cleveland staff was anchored by stalwarts Bob Feller, Bob Lemon, Early Wynn, and Mike Garcia, the best starting quartet in the major leagues. Yet it was Gene Bearden, a little, left-handed knuckleball pitcher (shades of Harry Brecheen!), who started the playoff game and won it, as the Indians earned the pennant with a 4-1 triumph. Once again, the Red Sox had come up one game short of making it to the World Series. Brickbats rained down on McCarthy, who had named little-used Denny Galehouse as his starter instead of the weary Parnell, his ace. He would not make that mistake again.

For the season, Ted's total of 25 homers was the lowest since his 1940 sophomore season, but he knocked in 127 runs and earned another batting title, his fourth in seven seasons, with a .369 average. Still, the Red Sox had missed the World Series by a single game. Next year, with the key players at their peaks, fans felt it must be different, had to be.

Boston may have felt the American League pennant was practically being handed to them when the 1949 season began—the 31-year-old Joe DiMaggio was on the disabled list. He'd had surgery on his right heel, and it wasn't healed. The pain remained in April, May, and well into June. It was not until June 28 at Fenway Park that Joe made his 1949 debut. The Red Sox, though, hadn't taken advantage of this gift from Providence. They were actually five games *behind* the Yankees when the series in Boston began.

Joe, who that season would catch the line-drive that ended his brother Dominic's 37-game hitting streak (still a Red Sox record), had what he later judged the "most satisfying" series in his life. The visitors swept all three games, with Joe singling and hitting a two-run homer in the first game, homering twice in the second game, and hitting a three-run homer in the third game. Were the Red Sox finished?

Not with Ted leading them. They chipped two games off the Yankees' lead in July, then during the next two months went 42-13. Even the Boston writers were praising Ted.

But not all the time: Stephens, hitting behind Ted, was having the best season of his career. In the last game of the season, with the pennant on the line, Ted was on second and Stephens lined a shot to left for a base hit. Ted rounded third but was held because of how quickly the ball had gotten to the outfield, and Ted was no Maury Wills on the base paths. Some mean-spirited Boston reporters later alleged that Ted resisted trying to score because if he had, Stephens would have captured the A.L. RBI title.

Red Sox players scoffed at such absurd allegations. As David Halberstam explained in his book, Ted and his teammates did indeed like one another, even after Ted's time in the majors ended.

Once again, as the season hurtled to a close, the Red Sox had a good chance of winning the American League pennant. Many fans believed that the game on September 25 would be the big showdown of 1949. Despite all the injuries the Yankees players had suffered and with a manager, Casey Stengel, untested in major league pennant races, New York had clung to first place day after weary day. With Joe

DiMaggio, sidelined again, this time by pneumonia, listening to the game at the hospital, the Yankees sent out the veteran Allie Reynolds against Mel Parnell, who was 15-3 at Fenway that season. Beating Boston at home and going two games up with a week left would be huge. But Parnell surrendered just one run, the equally worn-out Red Sox pushed four across—two on a seventh-inning two-run homer by Ted—and the teams were tied for first. It was Boston's ninth victory in a row.

The two teams hopped trains for the Bronx to make up for a game that had been rained out earlier in the season. Now the stakes were even higher. Certainly that was apparent to the 67,434 who piled into Yankee Stadium on the afternoon of the 26th. Was it too much to ask of the Sox to win 10 in a row? The Red Sox players may have reflected on their home-and-away record in 1949 and recognized it didn't bode well for winning at Yankee Stadium. They had been 61-16 at Fenway Park, but a paltry 35-42 on the road.

Sure enough, the Yankees jumped out to a 6-3 lead. But in the eighth inning, Boston tied it up and Johnny Pesky was dancing off third. Bobby Doerr executed the squeeze. Henrich, playing first, picked up the ball and tossed it to Ralph Houk. The catcher applied the tag, but Pesky was called safe. Stengel, his hair on fire, charged out of the dugout, but the call stood. Boston 7, New York 6. Ted had contributed to it with a hit and two walks. For the first time in the season, the Bronx Bombers were not atop the American League.

The next day, the Yankees won against the Philadelphia Athletics while the Red Sox took their 11th in a row, 6-4 over the compliant Senators. The Yankees won again on the 28th. In Washington, the Sox took a 1-0 lead into the ninth. This time, the Senators showed gumption, tying the game. They won when a weary Parnell uncorked a bases-loaded wild pitch. There was again a tie for first place.

Two days later, the Red Sox recovered with an 11–9 win in Washington, escaping a bases-loaded ninth with a game-ending double play. They collected only five hits, but the Senators were in a generous mood, issuing 14 walks (two to Ted) and committing three errors. When the Athletics downed the Yankees 4–1, Boston again had a one-game lead.

Entering the final weekend, Boston had gone 59–19 and needed only one more win in the final two games to be back in the World Series. "Sox and Parnell to Clinch Flag Today" the *Boston Herald* optimistically proclaimed on its Saturday, October 1, front page.

However, they would have to do it on Joe DiMaggio Day at Yankee Stadium. He had climbed out of his hospital bed to become a reclusive figure at his Manhattan apartment, 18 pounds lighter and still struggling to catch his breath. But now, with so much at stake, Joe couldn't stay out of the lineup.

As it had been on the 25th, the matchup was Reynolds versus Parnell, who by then had won 25 games, pitched 27 complete games (and would total 295 innings), had a 2.77 ERA, and had either started or been in the bullpen for the previous three weeks. No brotherly love now, Dominic, seeking to steal some of Joe's thunder, led off the game with a single. Pesky's bouncer should have been a double play, but Dominic took Rizzuto out at short before the relay to first. Ted singled, and a sacrifice fly by Stephens made the score 1-0. In the third inning, Reynolds walked Pesky, Williams, and Stephens, and Doerr's single made it 2-0. Joe Page came in and walked Al Zarilla, then he walked Billy Goodman. The Sox had a 4-0 lead going into the fourth.

With their leader ailing, it would have been easy for New York to fold, but they mustered a comeback in the fourth when Joe DiMaggio doubled to right and Hank Bauer drove him in with a single. Johnny Lindell singled, and Jerry Coleman's sac fly made the score 4–2. In the fifth, Rizzuto and Henrich singled, and Yogi Berra's single made it 4–3. Dobson was brought in the game to face Joe, who beat out an infield dribbler to load the bases with no one out. The Red Sox escaped with a tie score after a double play and a fly-out. The crusher for Boston was a two-out homer by Lindell in the eighth, and the Yankees hung on for a 5–4 win. Ted accounted for one of Boston's four hits.

Dramatically, the pennant came down to the final game. The winner of the American League's 154th contest would face the Brooklyn

Dodgers or the St. Louis Cardinals. (The National League race was going down to the final day too for a berth in the World Series.) Vic Raschi took the mound for New York and Ellis Kinder for the visiting team. The Boston right-hander surrendered a run in the first inning on a Rizzuto triple and a Henrich groundout, but he gave up nothing after that. The score was still 1–0 in the top of the eighth when McCarthy sent up pinch-hitter Tom Wright for Kinder, who walked. But Dominic DiMaggio bounced into a double play, and there was no threat. The Yankees' strategy to not let Ted beat them was to keep walking him.

New York capitalized against an exhausted Parnell, who had to be as surprised as anyone to still have an arm attached to his left shoulder. Henrich homered, making it 2-0 Yanks. After Berra singled, Tex Hughson came in to pitch. Before the inning ended, he had yielded a three-run double to Coleman. The box score might indicate this was a hard-hit ball that smashed off the outfield wall, but it was actually a tantalizing, twisting blooper over the first baseman's head with so much English that it spun to the wall and rolled down into the right-field corner. Inconceivable: would a dying quail double deny the Red Sox the pennant? (Many years later, Ted and Coleman would revisit this play—see Part VII.)

In the top of the ninth, the Red Sox were in a 5–0 hole. Pesky fouled out. Ted, of course, walked. Stephens singled. Doer tripled—a wheezing Joe was unable to catch up to the fly to center—to bring Ted and Stephens home. It was 5–2. Joe, spent, removed himself from the game, replaced by Cliff Mapes, who caught Zarilla's fly ball, and his throw home froze Doerr at third. Goodman singled, and the score was 5-3 with two outs. Henrich, drifting away from first, gloved a foul fly by Birdie Tebbetts, and the Yankees had won their 16th pennant, stunning even their own fans.

The Boston locker room was like a morgue. Stephens tried a couple of cheering-up comments, but nothing worked. "That phrase, 'You could hear a pin drop,' I never really knew what that kind of silence was like until after that game," the backup catcher Matt Batts recalled 63 years later.

The Red Sox had the dubious distinction of becoming the only team in major league history to finish a game out of first in two consecutive seasons—after playing 309 regular-season games during that period.

Once more, Ted had done all that could be asked of him, and in a few weeks he would have his second MVP Award to corroborate that. Playing in every game, in addition to sharing the RBI lead, Ted led the league in home runs with 43, he had walked 162 times, and scored a league-leading 150 runs. He missed another Triple Crown by the smallest of margins, a batting average of .3427 to the .3429 of George Kell of the Tigers. The Red Sox finished first in almost every offensive category . . . and it was not enough.

***

The Los Angeles Rams of the late 1960s and for much of the 1970s were not only a very good team, but a dynamic one, and there I was calling their games. After George Allen left to coach the Washington Redskins, he was replaced by Tommy Prothro, who was replaced by Chuck Knox. These coaches had a lot of weapons. The defense featured the "Fearsome Foursome"—Roosevelt Grier, Lamar Lundy, Merlin Olsen, and Deacon Jones—who over time were joined by Jack Pardee, Jack Youngblood, and Fred Dryer. On offense during those years were Roman Gabriel, Bernie Casey, Lawrence McCutcheon, Jack Snow, Harold Jackson, and Jackie Slater. Still, with all that talent and more, during my years in the broadcast booth, the Rams were just 3-7 in the playoffs and did not win a single Super Bowl. My last broadcast with the Rams was when the Minnesota Vikings, led by Chuck Foreman, beat them 14-10 at the Coliseum, again denying the Rams a shot at a championship.

Thankfully, my burgeoning career did not depend on that one Los Angeles team. I also announced the games of another local team, this one coached by a terrific man compiling an unmatchable career in college basketball—John Wooden and the UCLA Bruins. While

I had yet to meet the "Splendid Splinter," I was about to develop a wondrous relationship with the "Wizard of Westwood."

I called UCLA games on KTLA-TV from 1966 to 1975, encompassing the last nine seasons of Coach Wooden's unprecedented (and never-to-be-equaled) career. During those nine years, the Bruins won eight national championships. How incredibly fortunate I was to be a part of them. Think of it: eight national titles in nine years. Coach Wooden, with that wry smile, used to chide, "Enberg, you're pretty good." I loved doing football and baseball, but it was my connection with UCLA that shot me into the national limelight and triggered my move to NBC-TV in 1975. My entrée to the network was the success of UCLA. I rode the Wooden wave.

The home games were aired in Los Angeles at 11 p.m., on a tape delay. On the KTLA newscast just before the game, the final score was never flashed on the screen, and sportscasters warned viewers to cover their ears if they didn't want to know the final score. People sure watched—on Friday nights, for example, we outrated *The Tonight Show with Johnny Carson*. The center Bill Walton, UCLA's three-time National Player of the Year from 1972 to '74, told me years later the players couldn't wait to get back to their rooms to watch the replays. The more spectacular the game, the more times I said, "Oh my!" It was how the players gauged their performance.

I should point out that I did the Bruins games solo—without a color man. In those days, there was no producer. Venerable John Polich, a former hockey player, was the director, and, in essence, I was the producer. I basically did whatever I wanted, allowing me all the satisfaction borne of creative license. I was sure in the right place at the right time.

During John Wooden's last 10 years as coach, the team's home record at Pauley Pavilion was a phenomenal 149-2. Not surprisingly, given such success coupled with the improving technology, more games were televised nationally. And why not? That remarkable championship run of eight national titles, including seven in a row from 1967 to 1973, would be historic. The great bulk of the audience tuned in to see if anybody could beat this team. And when they did, it was a big, big deal. Wooden often kidded me that whenever I talked about the games I remembered the most, they were games that UCLA lost, and that was true, because you expected his team to always win. In fact, UCLA lost only 12 games—incredibly—in those nine years. Who wouldn't have been a good announcer?

One of those defeats remains the most exciting college basketball game I've ever seen, let alone called. It was the "Game of the Century"—one of the few times a contest has lived up to that sort of hype—on January 20, 1968. At 13-0 on the season, the Bruins traveled to Texas and the Astrodome to take on the also-undefeated, second-ranked Houston Cougars. In the previous season, the Bruins had defeated Houston to win yet another NCAA Championship. The 1968 match-up was broadcast nationally, with me and Basketball Hall of Famer Bob Pettit announcing for the syndicated network TV stations. UCLA was riding a 47-game winning streak—Lew Alcindor and his mates wanted to extend that, and Elvin Hayes and the talented Cougars of Guy Lewis, spurred by the all-time record crowd, aimed to stop it.

That they did. With the game tied 69–69, Hayes, who scored 39 points, was fouled, and he sank both free throws. The Bruins could not get a shot off, and as the buzzer sounded, the record crowd of 52,693 fans at the Astrodome went wild. The game was historic in many ways—largest crowd ever to pay to see a game, first time a collegiate game was played in a large domed arena, first time either a college or professional regular season game was televised nationally in prime time. And it was my first time on national television. How about that for a debut? Both teams went undefeated the rest of the season, and in the NCAA semifinals, UCLA crushed Houston 101–69 to regain the number 1 ranking and another national championship. It was absolute revenge.

Many experts point to the Michigan State-Indiana State NCAA title game in 1979—Magic Johnson versus Larry Bird—as the game that helped boost college basketball into the stratosphere. I disagree. I called that one, too, so I don't say this out of bias. The UCLA-Houston game 11 years earlier was the game that really showed the world how big college basketball could be. That was the rocket into outer space, appropriately in the home of NASA, Houston. The Bird and Magic finale then became the booster rocket.

What also made announcing UCLA games immensely special was my relationship with Coach Wooden, one of the most remarkable men I've ever met. Other than my own father, he was the greatest man I have ever known. His interests were so much wider than just basketball. He had a love of poetry—he had been a high school English teacher—and I think he could quote from every book ever written on Abraham Lincoln. As his players will tell you, he was a brilliant teacher, mentor, and certainly an inspiration. I found him to be the ultimate example of not only greatness, but goodness.

Of all his records—including 10 national titles, 88- and 47-game winning streaks, four unbeaten seasons, 19 conference titles, and the 149-2 record in Pauley Pavilion—to me the most significant was his team's phenomenal 38-game winning streak in the NCAA Tournament. That run of success lasted from 1964 until the double-overtime, three-point loss to eventual-champion North Carolina State in the 1974 national semifinal game. Think of it: 38 in a row, no softies, facing only teams good enough to be in the NCAA Tournament.

Couldn't just one championship be spared for the Boston Red Sox and the Kid?

***

A new decade could mean a fresh start for the Red Sox. For the most part, the team that had come oh so close the previous three seasons was still intact, and anchored by the "almost" Triple Crown winner. But as David Halberstam commented in his book about Ted, Pesky, Doerr, and Dominic DiMaggio, 1950 was really the last great season the four would experience together.

Ted would also reach his highest level in salary when Tom Yawkey offered him a $90,000 contract, with a $10,000 attendance bonus.

After a winter of hunting in Minnesota and Arkansas, then fishing back in the Everglades, accompanied by Doris and Bobby-Jo, the Kid responded by leading the American League in home runs and collecting 80 RBIs by the All-Star break. The Midsummer Classic was played at Comiskey Park, home of the Chicago White Sox. In the first inning, Ralph Kiner of the Pittsburgh Pirates hit a long fly to left. Moments later, Ted suffered the most serious injury of his career.

He had maintained for years that "they would never get me out of the game running into a wall. Running into walls was for guys looking for a short career." So what happens? Chasing Kiner's ball brought Ted into contact with the unforgiving left-field wall, with his elbow, especially, striking it hard. Ted did make the catch, but inning after inning the pain in his arm grew worse. The manager, Stengel, offered to take him out, but that wasn't Ted's way. Even with his elbow swelling to an impressive size, he managed a single in the eighth inning to give the American League the lead. It wasn't until the next day, back in Boston, that Ted went for x-rays. They showed a broken elbow, requiring a two-hour operation to set things right.

But the elbow never was quite right after that. Ted didn't know at the time that the surgeons thought his arm might be permanently disabled, which could mean the end of his career. However, after just two months he was back in the lineup, but never able to fully extend his arm. Ted played in only 89 games that 1950 season and with essentially one arm hit .317, the lowest average since his rookie season. Another reason for Richard Alan Enberg to want to be like his idol—with a broken elbow, playing in pain, literally batting one-armed, Theodore Samuel Williams outhit almost every other major league player. Talk about winning a fight with one hand tied behind your back!

The Red Sox tailed off late in the season, falling out of the pennant race. A frustrated Joe McCarthy didn't last until the end of the season. The Boston press was told he had resigned for health reasons. (McCarthy recovered, though he never managed again, and died in 1978, three months before his 91st birthday.)

There was a new manager, Steve O'Neill, and a new season of hope in 1951, when Ted rebounded to play in 148 games, and the Red Sox finished 20 games over .500 . . . but that was only good enough for third place. The Yankees, featuring a shy rookie named Mickey Mantle and with Joe DiMaggio wearing #5 for his final season, won their third straight American League pennant. O'Neill was fired. His replacement would be Ted's old nemesis, Lou Boudreau.

Ted Williams would not retire as a ballplayer until after the next decade had begun. During that time, he would fight in another war and in Boston earn two more batting titles. But he would be virtually alone—Doerr retired after the '51 season because of chronic back pain, Pesky would be gone the year after that, and early in the '53 season, Dominic DiMaggio would go from ballplayer to businessman. Now in his 30s, the Kid would find out the hard way that his career as a postseason contender was over.

***

I love baseball. It was the first professional sport I saw as a spectator, the sport I dreamed about playing on a major league level, and the sport I coached at the college level. I shared the love my dad and my maternal grandfather, Rudy Weiss, had for the game. I still have the two baseballs Grandpa Rudy willed me, autographed by the 1935 Detroit Tigers and 1935 Chicago White Sox.

Because I've called so many different sports, I'm often asked, "What is the most difficult sport to broadcast?"

No question, it's baseball. It's the most difficult, the most demanding, the most challenging, even the most exhausting. Why? Because it's the *longest* season, nearly 200 games, counting spring training. And it's the *slowest*-paced game, which pushes the announcer to work hard—particularly on the radio—to fill in those quiet moments when the pitcher is endlessly rubbing a wrinkle in the ball and the batter is loitering outside the batter's box.

Because the game moves at such a leisurely pace, the announcer is fully exposed. He not only needs to have plenty of anecdotes and stories at his disposal, but it's critical that he thoroughly understand the nuances of the game. In football, you can hide your lack of knowledge behind a good analyst. Basketball and hockey are so fast that you can conceal yourself within the hectic action. However, no sport exposes your lack of knowledge like baseball.

And I love it. Love the challenge. Even Ted Williams was surprised when I answered baseball was the most difficult. "Damn it," he said, I thought you were going to say basketball or one of those other sports." (I couldn't help thinking: did I actually win an argument with Ted Williams?)

Thus far in this book, there have been a couple of times that I have offered something Ted said to me directly. And for the most part, I have written about my professional career expanding to include a significant amount of coverage of football and basketball. But it was baseball that was closest to my heart, and incredibly, it was also in 1966, while I was doing Rams and Bruins games, that I began my broadcasting connection with major league baseball games. It was baseball that allowed me, three years later, to cross paths with that of my greatest sports hero.

PART V
Our Heroes

It might seem like a paradox that during the decade of the 1950s, as the Red Sox struggled to play .500 ball, Ted Williams finally became truly popular and appreciated in Boston. However, this wasn't due to Beantown fans accepting mediocrity as good enough. For the faithful, it was a very frustrating decade, which gave way to abysmal teams in the following decade until the "Impossible Dream" team of 1967, featuring Carl Yastrzemski and Jim Lonborg, made it to the World Series. With Ted, two things happened. One, for the second time, Ted went to war and became one of only a handful of players in major league history—Bob Feller, Yogi Berra, and Jerry Coleman immediately come to mind—to experience actual combat, and plenty of it. Two, fans finally came around to liking and respecting his effort and durability and desire to win. (Okay, there was that infamous "spitting" incident that I'll get to in Part VI.)

From age 11, Ted Williams was always my hero. But beginning in the 1950s, he was viewed by millions more, adults as well as youngsters, as an American hero. So, before covering that period that was both triumphant and frustrating, I'd like to discuss what being a hero is and why so many of us want and need them in our lives.

I'm no psychology expert by any means, but one of the most important lessons I've learned in broadcasting is to research and prepare. The topic of heroes has fascinated me for years, partly because I wanted to understand why Ted Williams was my enduring baseball idol. It turns out that many experts believe that we are born to have heroes. Scientists have found that babies are born with the abilities to learn language and numbers, to recognize faces, and to be drawn to people who are "moral," which I think means those who we sense have genuine goodness in them. We also at a very young age tend to view as heroes the people who take care of us. Often, these are parents, but they can be other caretakers, too.

For many children, a hero is someone who "saves the day," whether it be a character in a folk tale or a superhero in comic books and movies. Many adults transfer that to the police, firefighters, EMTs, etc. When we imagine a scenario that we're in trouble, or we really are in trouble, we hope a hero makes a timely arrival, just as we've read about or seen on a screen. And heroes do deeds "normal" people can't or won't do. They exhibit a special kind of courage, fortitude, resiliency, especially in difficult, even dangerous circumstances. For Ernest Hemingway, one of the most famous and influential writers of the 20th century, the heroes in such novels as *For Whom the Bell Tolls* and *The Old Man and the Sea* exhibited, as he called it, "grace under pressure."

Heroes can inspire us to become better people. From stories going back to Greek mythology and Homer's *The Iliad* and *The Odyssey*, all the way to modern times and today's print industry and broadcast industry and the Internet, we're presented with stories about men and women (and even children) who face danger, a moral quandary, or another very difficult or impossible situation, and they choose to do the right thing. This may involve high risk or even death, but essentially right is chosen over wrong and they act accordingly. Such stories inspire us to think that when push comes to shove, we will do the right thing, too: if that hero can do it, so can I.

Perhaps most of all, heroes offer an avenue toward wish fulfill-
ment. Some of us never quite give up our dreams, even ones that
began in childhood, but many of us reach a point when we begin to
understand and accept those dreams aren't about to become reality.
Hitting rocks while manning the fruit stand beside that lonely road
in rural Michigan, I must have burned billions of brain cells dreaming of my career as a major league baseball player. As I moved up the
education ladder and encountered more talented athletes, and then
broadcasting beckoned, I realized my dream would remain only an
ambitious hope. In Ted Williams, I saw someone who fulfilled his
dreams and, in a less direct way, mine.

Specifically, with heroes in sports we could sometimes be on risky
and shaky ground. The word "hero" gets tossed around much too
liberally in most sports, too often attributed to someone who has
achieved masterfully on the field but is decidedly unheroic off it. The
late-night talk show host Conan O'Brien, quoted in the "Sports On
the Couch" blog, once said, "A new report out of Chicago reveals that
the crime rate plummets during an NFL game. Mainly because the
most dangerous criminals are busy on the field."

This is an exaggeration, of course, and good for a laugh; but, for
better or for worse, we know more about "hero" athletes than we did
a generation and more ago. If you followed baseball in the 1910s and
'20s, you may have considered Ty Cobb a hero, never realizing he
relished his racist views. If you grew up in the Bronx in the 1950s and
'60s, your hero may have been Mickey Mantle, and for decades since
we've been informed about his crude behavior and struggle with alco-
hol. To how many millions was Tiger Woods a hero 10 years ago?
Just as seemingly unbeatable was the mythical Greek hero Achilles,
but his lesson is one of all heroes: Achilles. Vulnerable. Never perfect.

But I continue to believe the tarnished athlete-hero is more the
exception than the rule. There are many people playing baseball, football, basketball, soccer, hockey, golf, tennis, and other popular sports
who not only achieve on the field, court, or pitch, but do the hard and

thoughtful work to truly be heroic and set good examples to inspire youngsters.

One example is the Los Angeles Dodgers ace left-hander, Clayton Kershaw, who has campaigned to raise funds to build a school for an orphanage in Zambia, Africa. He has given $1 million of his own money to support a compound for many families and their children. Another example is Tennis Hall of Famer Andre Agassi, a career grand slam winner, and his Hall of Fame wife, Steffi Graf, who have supported with their time and finances the building of a prep academy in Las Vegas that provides a public charter school education to inner-city kids from kindergarten to 12th grade. (Their motto is "Work hard. Go to college. Change the world!") I can think of dozens more, such as Bill Walton and Drew Brees, who like Ted Williams did give back to children. Our sports heroes can exert great social influence and power and literally can impact generations.

For this book, I asked Walton for his insights on heroes and what they have meant to him. He responded with the following thoughts:

Heroes make things better. They're like forklifts and solar panels—they lift people and things up, putting them in a better place. I've been fortunate to have lots of heroes over the course of my now-64 years on this glorious planet. And like my life itself, my criteria for those heroes and their roles have changed tremendously, as has the culture that I am part of—a culture that today stresses, pushes, and demands qualitative binary decision making where everything has to be ranked, rated, compared, and measured. I choose not to go down that path of either/or, but rather to seek maximum enjoyment of yes, maybe, hopefully, and as much goodness as possible.

It's not about who's better, who's best; it's about who, and what, I choose to value, respect, imitate, and emulate. I've learned to dream outside the narrow confines of my own little life. From my parents, to my first coach, to my teachers, to the voices in my ear, to the people in my ever-expanding universe, I was chasing and living series of dreams based on hope, optimism, and joy. It was all so good, that it never crossed my mind that this was all about heroes. It was just the way it was.

In sports, I gravitated to Bill Russell and Muhammad Ali. On the social and political front, it was Bobby Kennedy and Martin Luther King Jr. My heroes are able to illuminate a path forward to a better place; they're capable of pulling a disparate team together; they define the terms of the conflict, making others play their game; they do what others can't and won't do; they hit first and initiate a relentless offensive attack; they understand, accept, and embrace that change, risk, failure, doubt, uncertainty, and hesitation are all part of everyday life and each and every endeavor and encounter; and they know how to effectively say NO—we're not going there, we're not doing that. My heroes have shaped the fire that burns inside of me . . . The same fire that was but a spark all those years ago . . . The same fire that danced a rhythm and a beat that reverberated a message of we can do better than this, and I'm willing to do something about it.

Invariably, all my heroes turned out to be nicer, kinder, and better human beings, with higher levels of humanity, ethical standards, and moral clarity, than I could have ever imagined or hoped for. When I started this journey, I didn't know anything about anything. Today, I know even less . . . but I do know who my heroes are and why. What I really know, though, is that I am who I am because of them.

Heroes have stood the test of time. They still do.

The future Hall of Fame quarterback Drew Brees of the New Orleans Saints is among the legion of those who idolized Ted. In fact, so much so, that he has collected precious memorabilia, including one of the few balls Ted kept as a personal treasure. In faded ink the baseball carries his inscription: "FIRST HOMER OFF BOB FELLER, MAY 14, 1946." (It's interesting how long it took Ted to take Feller deep—undoubtedly, one of the reasons he always praised the Cleveland right-hander for being one of the toughest ever to hit.) Brees also purchased at auction all of Ted's flight logs from both World War II and the Korean War. The logs contain dates of flights, types of aircraft (including the jet he crash-landed), various notes, and Ted's signature.

At the impressionable age of 10, Brees's admiration for Ted was spawned. Before going to Sunday School, he and his younger brother,

Reid, would watch an hour video, "Golden Greats of Baseball," which chronicled the baseball heroics and social impact of Jackie Robinson, Roberto Clemente, Hank Aaron, Joe DiMaggio, Nolan Ryan, and Ted, among others. "That's when I first fell in love with him, gravitated toward the Splendid Splinter," Drew told me. "I threw right and hit left just like him and wore his number 9 from Little League all the way through high school baseball. My dream, my goal, like Ted's, was to be the best hitter of all time in the Big Leagues, and with my brother I practiced and practiced. The dents in our garage door were evidence of my early efforts at hitting like my idol."

Meanwhile, Brees preferred number 14 for football and number 15 for basketball. They didn't have number 14 for football, so he continued to wear number 15 through high school and at Purdue University. When he was drafted by the San Diego (now Los Angeles) Chargers, someone else had 15, which gave him the excuse to ask for the number he really wanted, a perfect built-in excuse to grab 9.

"My admiration grew as I learned of Ted's sacrifice in order to serve for his country in two different wars," Drew said. "I was amazed. He risked his career, his life."

Despite playing his first five seasons in San Diego, he regrets never meeting Ted. Brees was a rookie in 2001, and Ted was desperately fading, dying in 2002. But the Super Bowl-champion quarterback has a treasured baseball and flight logs that adorn his office at home, reminders of the ballplayer and American hero that he wanted to be.

Studies show that regarding athletes as heroes peaks during adolescence. Some studies show that as many as 30 percent of kids in that age category, when asked who their heroes are, name athletes. Children are more likely to choose an idol who plays the sport they like most, then usually the same race and gender, then the athlete who plays the same position they do in baseball, basketball, etc. So, having an athlete as a hero is totally normal. Parents can understandably fret that their child's hero could turn out to have feet of clay. However, many players do earn the part of a hero and inspire children in the most positive way.

Ted Williams was skin and bones and still a teenager when he began playing professionally for the hometown San Diego Padres of the Pacific Coast League. *Courtesy of the National Baseball Hall of Fame and Museum.*

l won the American Association triple crown h the Minneapolis Millers; then he was on way to Boston. *Courtesy of the National eball Hall of Fame and Museum.*

As much as he loved hitting, Ted was happy to pitch, whether it be both ends of a Hoover High School doubleheader or against the Detroit Tigers in 1940. *Courtesy of the National Baseball Hall of Fame and Museum.*

The classic swing that would produce 521 home runs and awe youngsters and adults like me. *Courtesy of the National Baseball Hall of Fame and Museum.*

Before a fund-raiser exhibition game 1943, a Navy lieutenant known as the K lights the cigar of the Sultan of Swat, Ba Ruth. *Courtesy of the National Baseball H of Fame and Museum.*

The Cleveland Indians were the first to try (unsuccessfully) to frustrate Ted by employing a shift. Here the Cardinals try it in the 1946 World Series. *Courtesy of the National Baseball Hall of Fame and Museum.*

DiMaggio and Ted Williams were always ked as rivals during their playing days, d afterward, DiMaggio insisted on being roduced as the "greatest living ballplayer." rtesy of the National Baseball Hall of Fame d Museum.

Ted flew 39 missions as a combat pilot in Korea, and almost five years of his career were devoted to military service in two wars. *Courtesy of the National Baseball Hall of Fame and Museum.*

Ted was a huge supporter of the mmy Fund and would never say no to spending time with ill children, cluding this visit at Fenway Park in 953. *Courtesy of the Boston Red Sox.*

In his very last at-bat as a player, on September 28, 19[...] at Fenway Park, Ted, still with that classic swing, crushe[...] homer to right field. *Courtesy of the Boston Red Sox.*

For his entire 22-year career, Ted had a warm relationship with Tom Yawkey, owner of the Red Sox. *Courtesy of the National Baseball Hall of Fame and Museum.*

Ted, a first-ballot selection, is joined by fellow 1966 inductee Casey Stengel at the Natio[...] Baseball Hall of Fame ceremonies in Cooperstown. *Courtesy of the National Baseball Hall of Fa[...] and Museum.*

When his playing career was over, Ted could indulge fully in two other passions, hunting and fishing. *Courtesy of the National Baseball Hall of Fame and Museum.*

his first year with the Washington Senators, was voted Manager of the Year . . . but it downhill from there. *Courtesy of the National eball Hall of Fame and Museum.*

Here I am, at 16, with my brother, Dennis, proudly wearing my Armada (Michigan) town team uniform. *Courtesy of Dick Enberg.*

(Left) In 1957, I was the first voice of t[he] Indiana University Sports Network. [My] colleague, Phil Jones, would be a longti[me] CBS News correspondent. *Courtesy of D[ick] Enberg.*

(Right) There was never a dull moment—in the booth, at least—calling California Angels games in the 1970s with my Hall of Fame friend Don Drysdale. *Courtesy of Dick Enberg.*

I always enjoyed visits with broadcaster Vin Scully—not just a Dodgers legend, but a baseball legend. *Courtesy of Dick Enberg.*

On the set of *Spo[rts] Challenge*, a TV show I hosted, with guests Vince DiMaggio and T[ed's] Red Sox teamma[tes] Bobby Doerr, Dominic DiMag[gio], and Johnny Pesk[y]. *Courtesy of Dick Enberg.*

...anks to my friendship with him, Teddy ...lgame was kind enough to be my ...ystery guest" on *Sports Challenge*. With ...looks, he could have easily had his own ...show. *Courtesy of Dick Enberg.*

I treasured every moment spent with Ted, including here, when he was back in San Diego to be inducted into the Hall of Champions. *Courtesy of Dick Enberg.*

Broadcasting a San Diego Padres game in 2016 with my son Ted Enberg. Guess who he was named after! *Courtesy of Dick Enberg.*

Ted Williams as the centerpiece of the Athletic Wall of Honor at Hoover High in San Diego. *Courtesy of Tom Catlin.*

Ted Williams Field is just around the corner from his home in San Diego. Right field is less th 300 feet—no wonder he learned to hit lefty! *Courtesy of Tom Catlin.*

(Left) A young and handsome Ted with the build of a matinee idol poses on the steps of his family home on Utah Street in San Diego. *Courtesy of the San Diego History Center.*

(Above) I'm remembering baseball idol and friend ' Williams at the Utah Street ho *Courtesy of Tom Catlin.*

Okay, why for me, and thousands of others, was "Teddy Ballgame" my baseball idol? To toss out a few reasons, here's my pitch:

- **He was a dramatic player.** (Later, I would find out that he was an equally—if not more—dramatic person.) This book began with my remembrance of Ted hitting the home run in the 1946 All-Star Game that so fired the imagination of an 11-year-old boy. There were so many dramatic moments in his career—including his final swing, which is coming up in Part VIII—that the more appropriate question is: how could he not be a boy's hero? Baseball was the most popular sport in America at the time of my youth, and the Yankees and Red Sox were routinely on the big American League stage. When Joe DiMaggio and Ted Williams came through in the clutch, as they so often did, that was heroic stuff.

- **The magnitude of his achievements as a baseball player.** Ted retired after the 1960 season (meaning he played in four different decades), and no one since has matched his .344 lifetime average. (The mean major league batting average in 2017 was .255.) Those who came closest (all left-handed hitters) were Tony Gwynn at .339, Stan Musial at .331, and Rod Carew and Wade Boggs at .328. Gwynn, Carew, and Boggs did not come within shouting distance of 521 home runs and 1,839 runs batted in. Musial had 475 homers and 1,951 RBIs and was a great ballplayer (and person), but I can't help pointing out that he missed just one year because of military service while Ted missed four full seasons and some of a fifth.

- **That military service.** As mentioned previously, there were many ballplayers who served in the military. Very few, though, saw actual combat, and fewer still had to serve twice during two wars. Naturally, when Ted's career was over, he reflected on what the 4.5 lost seasons cost him, when he was 25 to 27 and 33 to 35 years of age. We can all do the math that he would have passed 600 home runs and 2,000 RBIs lifetime. Ted never complained. He did not cheerfully march off to war, but once he put on Uncle Sam's uniform, he did what he had to do for love of country. I like the way it was expressed to me by John Sununu, the three-term governor of New Hampshire: "Ted Williams was a great patriot and war hero who happened to be a great baseball hero."

- **Ted was very intelligent.** He read and studied voraciously. One of his favorite activities was to win debates, which he almost always did. He never attended college. Baseball was his college and graduate school, and he concentrated fiercely on it (and hunting and fishing too), but as the years went on, his interests expanded. He studied and argued politics with fervor, for example. The veteran Boston Red Sox trainer Jack Fadden was an unorthodox, brainy character who traveled the world. (After the Red Sox, he trained for Harvard University.) He had high regard for Ted and loved to tell tales about the Splendid Splinter. He viewed Ted as not only an immensely talented athlete, but an exceptional person. When I asked him about what if Ted had gone to college, Fadden replied, "He'd have also been an All-American football player; more than that, he'd have been Phi Beta Kappa."

- **Ted didn't have a racist bone in his body.** I'll discuss this further in the next section when the Red Sox finally added a black player to the roster, but for now: he was quick to embrace ballplayers of color in the major leagues. You can attribute this to his own Mexican descent, but it was more than that. Ted was a fair man, and he treated everyone the way they deserved to be treated. If you were a good ballplayer and worked at it, it didn't matter if you were pink or green. He was always quick to praise Satchel Paige, who eventually was inducted into the Baseball Hall of Fame, thanks in no small measure to Ted campaigning on behalf of black players, beginning with his own induction speech in Cooperstown.

- **He was a passionate man.** That could be something of an understatement because often it seemed like he spoke in capital letters. His voice was the equivalent of a sonic boom. He really cared about the things he cared about—baseball, of course, but also other people, especially "regular" folks. Some of his closest friends were ballplayers, such as Dominic DiMaggio and Bobby Doerr and Johnny Pesky, but he had strong, long-lasting friendships with people from all walks of life. The last thing Ted wanted when spending time doing charitable work was to be treated like a celebrity. No publicity. No photographers. No writers. He was helping kids because his heart told him it was the right thing to do.

- **Ted cared deeply about children.** Later, I'll get to his decades-long devotion to the Jimmy Fund in Boston; he raised million upon millions for programs that help sick kids. He did more than raise funds, though, spending countless hours with ailing children, but didn't want a word said about it. An aside: Think about an adult's first meeting with an ill child. Most would attempt to begin a conversation by asking for a name or favorite person or player. Ted's opening was brilliant: "What's your pet's name?" What kid wouldn't relax with a good answer about a pet and be willing to continue?

- **He was damn handsome.** Ted may have been scrawny and awkward at 17 but with age and experience acquired John Wayne-like good looks. If he had gone to Hollywood, he would have been a star in the 1940s and '50s alongside Wayne, Robert Mitchum, Kirk Douglas, and Burt Lancaster.

- **He was supremely confident.** Not surprisingly, given his brawny good looks and magnificent deeds, there was a heroic swagger about him. He didn't need to apologize for how good he was and how great he wanted to be. Yet, to his credit, he didn't deny or flaunt it. The constant supportive evidence was the sound created when Williams made contact with that round ball with a round bat. One of my favorite Ted anecdotes comes from the 1950s. It involves Pedro Ramos early in his career, pitching for the Washington Senators. It sure was a big moment for the young right-hander when he struck Ted out. He rolled the ball into the Washington dugout to keep as a souvenir. To make it even more special, after the game Ramos approached Ted in the clubhouse and asked him to sign it. Steam blew out of Ted's ears and a verbal Vesuvius was seconds away, but then he saw how scared the Cuban rookie looked and said, "Oh, all right, give me the goddamn ball." Two weeks later the Red Sox and Senators were playing each other and again Ted came up to face Ramos. A very different result this time—there was the crack of a bat and the ball hurtled out to deep right field, landing in the stands. Rounding first, Ted called to Ramos, "I'll sign that son of a bitch too if you can ever find it."

- **Ted was unfailingly honest.** This often got him into trouble, especially with the Boston sportswriters, when keeping his mouth shut or at least being tactful would have been the easy way out. But he called them as he saw them. You always knew where you stood with Ted Williams. As Bobby Knight told me, "Ted didn't B.S. anyone. If he said it, he meant it." Bobby's voice cracked a bit when he added, "It's one of the most meaningful relationships of my entire life, to get to know him. I'm proud that I can actually say he was a friend. I can hear him now starting a friendly yet calculated argument, 'Goddamn Coach...' That's how it would always start."

- **Uncommon talent.** Without it, the hero system vaporizes. We crave and cheer the uncommon, the extraordinary. That's what Ted Williams was all about. Rare. He was the greatest hitter of my lifetime.

And those are the reasons why I wanted to be Ted Williams. And those are the qualities while doing research for this book that reinforce my respect and admiration for Teddy Ballgame all the more.

I am fully aware, as are most people who saw Ted as a hero, that like Achilles and his heel, Ted had flaws. His personality ranged from crude and caustic to bold and boyish. The drive to perfection created a wide range of behavior that included frustration and anger when the day produced nothing but pop-ups and strike three. Okay. When I go to the ice cream shop, I'm seeking much more than vanilla; I'm looking for flavors and nuts. (I'm never disappointed with Butter Pecan or Chocolate Almond Fudge.) So it is with our idols. Vanilla personalities are not nearly as appealing. We all have our flaws, failings, and vulnerabilities. They don't have to detract. They make us human. Like you and me. And being human was being Ted Williams.

I'm reminded of a cartoon in my youth. It features a lifetime .220 hitter who has heard few cheers to compensate for the chorus of boos at his meager performance. He goes to spring training after a winter's experiment with his swing, making major adjustments. Whatever he did, worked. He goes through the exhibition season without making a single out and he's the talk of baseball. The team heads north and the streak continues. After two weeks he's still hitting a thousand ... and the fans begin to boo him. They boo louder and louder with each hit. They can't stand someone who won't make an out. No one hits one thousand. No one is absolutely perfect. No one. Not even Ted.

Even though it has been almost two decades since Ted died, there are many players today who view him as a hero. Joey Votto of the Cincinnati Reds has admired Ted since his teenage years in Toronto. As a kid, he would practice, return home to study Ted's books on hitting, and return to practice to work on what he had read. His admiration of Ted grew as he learned more of his military service and the almost five years of baseball denied because of it.

Votto, who earned the National League's Most Valuable Player award in 2010, felt that Ted was the ultimate power hitter of his time. Votto wears #19 on his back, the same number Ted wore as a 17-year-old high school senior, when he signed with the Pacific Coast League San Diego Padres. (The late Tony Gwynn, another admirer and a San Diego Padre, also wore 19.) Votto, like Ted, is a selective hitter, annually leading the National League in walks. Some Cincinnati fans have been critical, complaining that he walks too much when he's being paid to hit the ball. Ted went through the same negative treatment. But don't forget, Ted's first rule was to get a good pitch to hit, not a *bad* pitch to hit. Of today's top players, Votto has seemed to learn from his own teenage Ted Williams studies as well as any modern hitter. Incidentally, a copy of Ted's *The Science of Hitting* is a constant companion for Votto, home and away.

Unfortunately for the Reds star, he didn't have an opportunity to meet his baseball hero. There is something about that experience that is transforming. I certainly felt it with Ted. When researching *Summer of '49*, David Halberstam interviewed Ted and reported, "My day with him was magical." Afterward, the author was trying to figure why, at age 54, he felt 12 years old again meeting "a great figure of my childhood." He concluded it was because Ted Williams "gave so much. It was the unique quality of the energy level—I have rarely seen it matched. He gave more than he took. In the age of cool, he was the least cool of heroes. Rather, he was a big kid who had never aged and had no intention of aging; I was alternately dazzled and almost exhausted by his energy and his gift for life.

"I have this view of him now, and it was beginning to form back then, that it had all come around to him because he was not a modern man, had always gone his own way, always outside the bounds of contemporary society, and had been so absolutely true to himself."

Yes, if only I could be like Ted Williams.

PART VI

The Aging Gladiator

As 1952 began, Ted Williams thought rumors that he would be called back into the Marine Corps were ridiculous. Sure, the Korean War was raging, but he had already served three years in the military. Incredibly, though, in January he was moved from the list of inactive reservists to active duty. Still, hoping this might just be a bad dream, Ted went to spring training. One silver lining once the team went north to Boston was he felt an extra and uncommon warmth from the fans, given the fact that he'd been called up twice already. In turn, he hoped that there'd be a politician who might fight the injustice.

None of them did. Nothing changed when, during his physical, he presented the damaged arm from crashing into the wall. The doctor patted it and said, "You're okay."

Only six games into the season, Ted took off his #9 uniform and put on the uniform of a captain in the Marine Corps. By doing so, as Bill Nowlin points out in *Ted Williams at War*, he went from an annual salary of $100,000 to $7,500. Before he left Boston, there were to be ceremonies honoring Ted. The only battle "Colonel" Dave Egan fought was with the bottle, yet he had the gall to write, "Why are we having a day for *this* guy?" On this matter, he was not in tune with most of the Boston readers and fans of the Red Sox. The city declared Ted Williams Day with festivities at Fenway Park before the game against the Detroit Tigers.

He was presented with a Cadillac and a donation made in his name to the Jimmy Fund. (More about this in the next section.) Most surprising and rewarding was the "Ted Williams Memory Book," containing the signatures of 400,000 fans.

Ted took his cap out of his back pocket and pointed it at the left-field stands where his most persistent critics sat. "This is the greatest day of my life," he told the cheering crowd. "I'll always remember it. It is a day every ballplayer looks for, and one I thought I'd never have." This was a poignant admission coming from one of the best players ever.

As usual, Ted's most dramatic response was with his bat. There were two outs in the bottom of the seventh inning with the score 3-3 when Ted stepped to the plate to face Detroit's Dizzy Trout. Dominic DiMaggio was on base for what might be Ted's last time at bat ever. Trout tossed a curve, and Ted deposited it into the right-field bull-pen. The Red Sox held on for the 5-3 victory. Because he had gone 4-for-10, however brief, Ted had his second .400 season.

That night, uncharacteristically, Ted hosted a party, at the Hotel Kenmore. He invited his kind of people—not celebrities, but cab drivers, bellhops, cops, bartenders, and the team's bat boys. He reflected about his game-winning wallop, "I had to think at the time that it was my last home run in big league baseball. I was thirty-three years old. I would be thirty-five when I got back. Chances were I wouldn't play again."

Within days, he was on his way to Willow Grove, Pennsylvania, for eight weeks of training. Given that he hadn't flown a plane in seven years on top of not having ever flown a fighter jet, the odds weren't great that Ted would return from Korea in one piece, if at all. When he was deemed ready as a jet fighter pilot, Ted was shipped out, first to Tokyo, then to the port city of Pohang in Korea. The base there was 180 miles from the front lines of the United Nations forces. In mid-February 1953, instead of being on his way to Sarasota for spring training, Ted flew his first combat missions. As Bill Nowlin put it in *Ted Williams at War,* "Instead of looking at the lineup to see where he'd be batting that day, Captain Williams would be checking the Ready Room board to confirm his combat assignment." The third assignment, on February 16, came very close to being his last.

After unloading his bombs at the target—a tank training school 15 miles south of the North Korean capital Pyongyang—emergency lights in the cockpit began flashing. Ted's jet had been hit by a small arms fire without him realizing it. He tried to alert his squadron of a hydraulic leak, but his radio was out. Another pilot, Larry Hawkins, observed that the stricken jet was streaming fluid, which he believed was fuel. Hawkins used hand signals to tell Ted to follow him. They headed for home, but it seemed highly unlikely that the damaged jet would make it. Ted refused to eject because he was tall and stocky and could barely fit into the cockpit, and he had no confidence that he would successfully be hurled out.

After 15 minutes, it became clear that Ted wasn't going to make it. Any moment, his jet could explode. Hawkins led Ted to the nearest base, a rather crude one. He was at 300 feet and preparing for an emergency landing on a 9000-foot dirt runway.

By now, Ted had nothing—no brakes, no flaps, and no landing gear. All he had was sheer determination. He put the jet down on the runway, and the jet skidded to a stop with less than a thousand feet to spare. Ted clambered out of the cockpit as fire crews hosed the craft down with foam. Not that this did any good. An observer of Ted's near-death experience was Major John Glenn, who had joined the VMF-311 squadron only the day before. In a 1996 interview with Nowlin, Senator Glenn recalled, "It slid up the runway and he jumped out of the cockpit and ran off and stood there watching it melt down. He was just lucky that thing didn't blow."

The jet was completely destroyed. Ted's commanding officer offered him time off after the close call. But Ted knew his squadron was short of pilots. He was back in the air the next day.

Of the 39 combat missions Ted flew, about a dozen were as wingman to Glenn, who was also a Marine Corps reservist and had served during World War II. The two formed an immediate friendship. Until his death in 2016, Glenn praised Ted as a pilot and a person. He was not one to pass out cheap compliments, especially about men with whom he served in the Marine Corps. So, it really meant something when years later, Senator Glenn said, "Ted was the best pilot I've ever been around."

For his part, Ted would say about being the future astronaut's wing man, "I never was very good around instruments and admit I was a little scared by that shortcoming. I hung on to Glenn like glue."

Much of the time that Ted fought in Korea, he was sick with respiratory problems. A stay on a hospital ship being given fluids intravenously did not cure him and only made him less sick for a short period of time. He never shirked a mission, though, but finally, Ted was so sick with pneumonia that even he had to stand down. His 39th and last combat mission was on June 10. A dozen jets of the VMF-311 squadron took off that morning and attacked enemy positions at Tangjang-ni.

A few days later, he was ordered to Japan for further treatment. For Captain Ted Williams, Marine Corps pilot, the Korean War was over. Though very proud of his service in World War II as well as in Korea, Ted would always insist, "I was no hero." He sure was to me and millions of other people! Whether or not he ever hit another home run, his title as a hero was indelibly secure.

When Ted returned to the US, recuperating in San Francisco, he received a call from Commissioner Ford Frick inviting him to throw out the first ball at the 1953 All-Star Game in Cincinnati. He received a big ovation from the crowd and wondered how long it would be before he'd be involved in more than just a ceremonial first pitch. Back in Boston, Ted discovered that Johnny Orlando had three brand-new

#9 uniforms waiting for him, and that his locker had been off-limits to everyone while he was at war. Looking around, Ted could see that Manager Lou Boudreau had made good on his vow to retool the Red Sox lineup via a youth movement.

Bobby Doerr was gone, retired with the bad back, to renew life in Oregon. Johnny Pesky was gone, too. "The Needle," heartbroken, had been traded to the Tigers during the 1952 season. Pesky wasn't the only one who was devastated by the trade. One of my Detroit favorites, George Kell, went to the Red Sox (along with Hoot Evers, Dizzy Trout, and Johnny Lipon). Kell would later return to the Tigers as their TV play-by-play announcer. And "Dommie" was gone, too. Though still arguably the best center fielder in the American League and having batted .294 the previous season, at age 36 and playing only three games that spring, DiMaggio had reluctantly accepted that Boudreau's plans did not include him and he retired.

Ted's first game back in early August 1953 was as a pinch-hitter in Washington, and he popped out. But Ted's flair for the dramatic came through again. The following Sunday, August 9 (there's that number again), at Fenway Park, he blasted a homer as a pinch hitter—his second dinger in as many at-bats. In fact, in the next 37 games, Ted hit an amazing .407 with 13 home runs in just 91 at-bats, which averaged out to a homer every seven times up, all from a jet pilot who had been away from baseball for a season and a half. Best hitter ever? I rest my case.

While writing this book, I spoke to Del Wilbur Jr., who grew up a baseball kid, thanks in large part to his father being a reserve catcher in the major leagues for 10 years (including 1952-54 with the Boston Red Sox) and a coach and scout for another 40 years. Del Jr. recalls when he was 10 years old visiting the home locker room at Fenway Park soon after Ted returned from Korea:

To get to my dad's locker I had to walk by Ted's cubicle. The clubhouse was small and Ted's voice was large, so I heard it all. I must have heard a

half-dozen words that I hadn't heard before, including that the writers were
"c**********." I asked my dad what that meant, and he said he'd tell me later.
Ted may have hated the writers, but he loved kids. He was always nice to me
and the sons of other players and coaches.

One day I was shagging balls in the outfield while he was taking extra
batting practice, alone. When we got to the dugout he bought me a Coca-
Cola and invited me to sit down, saying, "Let's talk baseball." He yelled to the
clubhouse guy, "What's the biggest coin you can find?" He was given a half-
dollar. He then lifts his bat to cross over his knees, takes the coin, and sets it on
the sweet spot. He showed me the marks he had just made when hitting for a
half-hour. The coin covered EVERY mark. Every single mark hidden, masked
behind the coin. He had made contact in the same sweet spot for half an hour.
Ted told me, "That's what you want to do when you're hitting."

In 1989, my father celebrated his 70th birthday. I wrote letters to some
of his old teammates, asking if they would send a note or card to put in a
scrapbook. Ted sent a telegram: "This must be a great day celebrating your
70th birthday. I know it will be a happy time for you and your many friends.
I wish I could have had a hitter of your caliber behind me the 23 years of my
career. I would have hit more home runs. You're a great guy in my book and
I wish you the very best always. Sincerely, Ted Williams."

My dad died within a month of Ted in 2002. Both were battling fading
health in 2000. Big Del had prostate cancer. I asked several former teammates and friends to give him a call, pick up his spirits. A bunch of guys
obliged. Ted told me, "Fuckin' yes, I'll call right now." And Ted, with his
own serious health issues, did. Is this the bad guy the press loved to criticize?

Understandably, everyone predicted that a rejuvenated and seemingly ageless Ted Williams would tear up the American League in the
1954 season . . . but it sure didn't start out that way. Spring training
had hardly begun when Ted fell chasing a fly ball and broke his collarbone. This was no simple injury—the collarbone had to be rebuilt
with a four-inch stainless-steel pin that would remain in his shoulder
for the rest of his life. Best case scenario: if everything healed okay,
Ted would miss six weeks, or 36 games. He was so despondent that

in an article in the *Saturday Evening Post*, he announced that when the season ended, so would his career. His marriage ended, too. Things had not been going so well with Doris before he was shipped out to Korea, and they didn't get better after he returned. That May, divorce papers were filed.

Ted rushed his way back in the lineup. The collarbone still pained him when he made his '54 season debut on May 7. But this was at Briggs Stadium, so it didn't matter—he not only played both ends of a double-header, but went a blistering 8-for-9. He played in every game afterward, and the 35-year-old with a bum wing wound up batting .345. If he'd had enough at-bats, this would have qualified for a fifth AL batting title. Ted decided not to retire.

But under Boudreau, the Red Sox were not an emerging team but one barely treading water. In 1952, Boston had finished in sixth place, two games under .500. Fourth place in 1953 was a bit better, but they finished 16 games behind the despised Yankees. The cast of players around Ted was not anywhere close in talent or stature. Some Boston reporters came to refer to each day's starting lineup as "Ted Williams and the Seven Dwarves." Nevertheless, Ted had already shown more than once he wasn't a quitter. If indeed he carried the weight of the offense and was the major reason why fans kept coming to Fenway Park, he would just go out there every game and do his job.

***

My first involvement with the Los Angeles Angels (later to become the California Angels) came in March 1966, before I took on the Bruins and Rams broadcasting jobs. I was the host and producer of the half-hour pre- and postgame shows on KTLA, which televised 40 Angels games each season. Our pregame show usually had three eight-minute interviews. My debut was in Palm Springs, where the Angels were playing the Chicago Cubs on a spring training weekend. The Angels manager, Bill Rigney, and young outfielder Rick Reichardt, billed by some as the next Mickey Mantle, agreed to be on that first show. We needed someone from the Cubs, and Leo Durocher, the fiery, legendary manager, was the obvious choice. When I told our venerable director John Polich and producer Bob Speck that I planned to ask Durocher, they grimaced and said he wouldn't do it: "He'll want to be paid."

Well, that was all the bait I needed. An hour and a half before the game, I walked onto the field as the Cubs took batting practice. Durocher was leaning on the cage, watching his team, and I slowly edged my way closer and closer, until I was standing at his side.

"Skip," I said, "I'm Dick Enberg, the new announcer with the Angels, and I would like to invite you to be a guest on my first pregame show today."

Durocher was completely unimpressed, not even bothering to look my way.

I pushed on. "Bill Rigney and Rick Reichardt have already agreed to be guests, and it would make the show perfect if you were on, too. You really should be the other guest."

The Cubs' manager finally turned to look at me. "It'll cost you a grand," he snapped.

"I won't make $1,000 all of spring training," I countered, "but I'll buy you a bottle of whiskey."

Durocher hesitated—and then smiled. "You got me, kid."

For the next three years, I continued to host the regular season pre- and postgame shows from the KTLA studios in Hollywood. After the game, we showed highlights, gave the other scores, and had an inside baseball segment where, as a former coach, I took a couple of plays and analyzed them. We had a seven-foot metal scoreboard on the set that was big enough for all the games, and often I updated it myself, using magnetic team names and numbers. At the time it was basically a one-man production. I had no studio assistance.

One fateful day, it all came apart. I was Lucille Ball on the chocolate assembly line. As I arrived in the studio to update the magnetic scoreboard, I was hit with not one, but several games ending, simultaneously. Over the intercom, the director, noting my dilemma, barked,

"One minute," as he counted me to the on-air opening of the show. Nervously, I dropped a couple final numbers trying to get them on the board. "20 seconds." I barely scraped them up and let the magnets go to work. "10 seconds." I sprinted to my chair as the countdown hit, "3-2-1." Out of breath, I gave my best TV smile and beamed, "Hello, everyone, what an Angels win. We have highlights, a couple great defensive plays, and all the major-league scores for you on our Angels postgame show."

In those days, there was no earpiece connection for the control room to give me direction. It was a one-camera operation, and the camera operator at this point was peeking out behind his monster-sized device, gesturing with several emphatic points at me. Something was wrong, but I didn't know what, so I continued to soldier on. Finally, it hit me. In my haste, I had failed to put on my lavalier microphone. I was sitting on it. No chance to call a time-out, so live on camera, I just stood up, reached behind me, pulled out the mic and clipped it on my jacket, and blushingly continued. You can imagine the fan mail that I received, most of it with a common theme, "Enberg, you never sounded better." So no matter what you may have heard, if nothing else in my career, Dick Enberg can claim that he invented the "rectal microphone."

As the 1968 baseball season ended, I was quite content with my busy broadcasting life, which included doing nightly sports news, boxing, UCLA Bruins basketball, LA Rams football, and Angels pre- and postgame shows. Suddenly, I had a huge decision to make. Buddy Blattner, the lead announcer for the Angels on radio and television since 1962, received an offer to be the No. 1 announcer for the expansion Kansas City Royals. Having grown up in the Midwest, he decided to return home. I was offered the job. It was only many years later that I learned Gene Autry, who owned KMPC, KTLA, and the Angels, pushed for me to get the lead announcer position. I was 34.

As much as I love baseball, at first I resisted. Not only would I have to give up the nightly news and boxing, but by then my daughter, Jennifer, was six and my son, Andrew, was three. I knew baseball would take me away from home much more—for 81 games on the road, plus spring training. As I hesitated at the offer, the KTLA general manager, Doug Finley, asked me a crucial question: "Don't you want to be remembered as one of the great announcers someday?"

"Of course, who wouldn't?" I replied.

"Well, name me one great announcer who did not do baseball."

In thinking of outstanding announcers in my time—Red Barber, Mel Allen, Vin Scully, Van Patrick, Curt Gowdy, Ernie Harwell, Ken Coleman, Chuck Thompson—I realized they had all called baseball. Finley suggested that I try it for a year. He promised me that if it didn't work out after one season, I could come back to KTLA and resume doing boxing, news, and other assignments. We agreed on a one-year trial.

Thankfully, that one-year audition turned into nine (9!) years. The Angels were not a good ball club. But I learned a lot, right from the start. Before my first regular-season game that year (1969), Fred Haney, the voice of the Angels and Stars I had listened to broadcasting Pacific Coast League games when I was a boy in the San Fernando Valley, suddenly appeared in my Anaheim Stadium booth. Now, after managing the Milwaukee Braves to two World Series appearances (and one championship), he was the Angels' first general manager.

"I've been listening to you during spring training," Haney said, "and I know you're going to do a good job for us. But let me give you one piece of advice. As an announcer, just report the ball. Don't tell me what you hope the ball will do, or what you think the ball will do. Report the ball and you'll be fine." Then he walked out.

It was sage advice in many ways. For years, when I ran out of material and action was at a standstill, I'd just find the ball and describe what it was doing: "The pitcher hides the ball behind his back, takes the catcher's sign, backs off the rubber, rubs up the ball, stares in, nods, grips, winds, and throws . . ." and naturally kept tracking the ball, wherever it went after that.

My years with the Angels also allowed me to get to know two remarkable people. One was Don Drysdale, the great Dodgers pitcher and Hall of Famer. He was broadcasting for the Texas Rangers when

KMPC decided to replace Don Wells as the Angels No. 2 announcer. It made sense to hire a man who had starred in Los Angeles as a player his entire career. It was definitely a major stroke of luck for me.

Drysdale was a major reason why I lasted so long with the Angels. The dog days in baseball are real, particularly in August with a losing team. But there was never a dog day working with Don. Every day was a great day. Forever positive, he always made the day fun. He wouldn't let you get down. We worked together for six years, and we laughed together for six years.

Another reason why I lasted so long was thanks to Gene Autry. He had a fabulously successful career as a movie and radio-TV star and entertainer, but that simple little Christmas song, "Rudolph the Red-Nosed Reindeer," made him almost more money than any other profitable endeavors. (Though originally he didn't even like the song, his first wife, Ina, did and talked him into recording it.)

One spring training, he invited all of the players, their wives, children, and the media to a barbecue around the pool at the Gene Autry Hotel in Palm Springs. The Sons of the Pioneers, a group of western singers, provided the entertainment. As the evening progressed, the crowd begged Gene to sing a song. He was in his 60s then and no longer had the buttery-smooth, golden voice of his youth. But he finally conceded and warbled a couple of songs, and at the request of several big-eyed kids, he sang "Rudolph the Red-Nose Reindeer." As he sang, he got better and better. The hoarseness left his voice. And he couldn't have been more brilliant. He became younger before our spellbound eyes and ears.

But above all during those years calling Mr. Autry's games in Los Angeles, I finally was able to meet my baseball hero—I was an Angel, and he was a Senator.

***

When the 1955 season began, Lou Boudreau was gone, exiled to become skipper of the lowly Kansas City Athletics. Years later, Dick

Flavin famously commented that the former shortstop "did more damage to the Red Sox as their manager than he ever did playing against us in an Indians uniform."

Boudreau was replaced by Pinky Higgins, who certainly didn't invite any comparisons with Casey Stengel. Joe Cronin was still the general manager, but he had lost his touch in finding talent, either in the farm system or on other teams. But there was a bigger reason than that for the Boston Red Sox becoming less competitive: A monumental blunder, they had refused to sign black players. Back in the mid-1940s, Jackie Robinson had tried out, and the franchise rejected him. They had also passed on Willie Mays. (Oh my!) There was an iron-fisted policy from Tom Yawkey on down that the faces of the Red Sox were to remain white. They would be the last of the major league teams to integrate, and this would prove to be catastrophic for the franchise.

So, in the 1950s, as Mays, Henry Aaron, Willie McCovey, Elston Howard, and other gifted African-American players emerged as All-Stars, the hold-out Red Sox drifted along in mediocrity. In 1954, they finished a whopping 42 games out of first place. (Granted, the Cleveland Indians with Larry Doby and Luke Easter lapped the field with 111 victories.) The best Boston could do the following season was fourth place. In 1956, it was down to seventh place. Then the next year, third place but 16 games behind New York. In 1958, they "improved," finishing 13 games behind the Yankees.

As far as pennant races are concerned, the Red Sox had become irrelevant. When they finally promoted a black player, infielder Pumpsie Green, in 1959, that could not rid the organization of its malaise as Boston sank to fifth place, again under .500.

Nevertheless, no one had given Ted Williams the memo that it was okay to just punch the clock and go home. In his late 30s, at 40, and beyond, Teddy Ballgame put on a heck of a show. He was getting paid very well, and he earned every line-drive penny of it. In 1955, he hit .356. The following year, only Mickey Mantle's .365 beat his .345.

Yet most astonishing was the 1957 season. Ted would turn 39 before it was over. He had very little support in the lineup, so most opposing pitchers weren't going to be dumb enough to give him any-thing good to hit. And yet, he batted a stunning .388 and earned his fifth AL title. If Ted's old legs had turned close outs at first into hits, he would have topped .400. He told me with full conviction that he couldn't remember getting a "leg hit." That season, if he had beaten out just seven infield dribblers, he'd have batted .400, again. As it was, he batted .403 in the season's last 55 games. He also belted 38 home runs, and his slugging percentage of .731 was Ted's best since 1941. Though he hit only .328 at age 40 the next season, it was good enough for a sixth title. Dramatically, he clinched it the final day of the season by going 3-for-4 and nosing out teammate Pete Runnels.

Along the way, the Fenway fans fully came to appreciate and pull for Ted Williams. No doubt, some fans remembered what had been dubbed "Great Expectorations," when after being booed for commit-ting an error, Ted spat repeatedly toward the Fenway Park fans. Sure, Ted wasn't about to forget that during his divorce in 1955 a few of the Boston newspapers ran a "box score" on the money, the house, the car, and "Mrs. Ed's" custody of Bobby-Jo. But now, all was forgiven, and finally it looked like a two-way street.

The day the 1958 season ended, Ted flew to Maine, where a fellow angler came up to the batting champ and told him he was an excellent fisherman, too. Talking to a Boston writer one day, Ted proclaimed, "Ain't no one in heaven or earth ever knew more about fishing."

"Sure there is," responded the writer.

"Oh, yeah? Who?"

"Well, God made the fish."

"Yeah, alright," Ted allowed. "But you sure had to go pretty far back."

Life had gotten pretty good: "Gee, here I am forty years old and feeling like I could go on forever."

Instead, the following season it looked like Ted Williams was all washed up. In the spring, he hurt his neck taking practice swings and wound up in traction with a pinched nerve. Then he had, by his own admission, "a miserable year." He couldn't wait for it to be over, and when it was, the Kid, now 41, had batted an incomprehensible .254

and slugged only 10 home runs. Also during that dismal season, Ted's brother, Danny, who had struggled in the shadow of his big brother including scrapes with the law, died of leukemia. He was only 39. (The same disease would claim Ted's only son, John-Henry, when he too was in his late 30s.)

However, one typical Ted achievement in the 1959 season had taken place during spring training, when he made sure others on the Boston club saw its superstar greet the team's first black player, Pumpsie Green. The Red Sox had moved their spring training site from Sarasota to Scottsdale, Arizona, where Ted had a chance to introduce himself to Green and include him in his warm-ups, as well.

Green was demoted to the minors, but when he was called up during the season, Ted resumed their pregame connection. This time, he wanted not only his teammates to see him welcome a black player, but the Boston fans, too. When the team warmed up in front of their dugout before each game, it was Ted who played catch with Pumpsie.

The following spring, the Red Sox and Indians left camp in Arizona to play an exhibition game in New Orleans before going on to Boston and Cleveland. Each team had two black players—Green and pitcher Earl Wilson with the BoSox, and pitcher Jim "Mudcat" Grant and first baseman Vic Power with the Indians. Because New Orleans was a segregated city, while the rest of the two teams piled on buses, the four black players took a cab to a blacks-only hotel. Once there, they realized their bags had gone with the buses. Grant was nominated to grab a cab to retrieve them. However, the doorman wouldn't even let him into the lobby, where the four team bags had been dumped. Grant argued he could see the bags through the door and it would take just a minute to bring them out to the street, but the doorman vehemently refused: "We let you in and all the other n****** will want to follow." Out of nowhere came Ted. He quickly assessed the situation and bellowed at the doorman, "Go get the fucking bags and put them in a fucking taxi!" The terrified doorman couldn't do this fast enough. "Yes sir, Mr. Williams." Imagine how that resonated in the black baseball community.

After the 1959 season concluded, Red Sox owner Tom Yawkey said to Ted, "I think you ought to quit." Dick O'Connell, who had replaced Joe Cronin as the general manager (Cronin would become president of the American League), was more encouraging, offering Ted a 1960 contract for the same $125,000 he'd been paid for the just-concluded season. Ted signed it—after insisting on a $35,000 pay cut, explaining, "I was no $100,000 ballplayer." He had too much integrity to take what was essentially the fans' money for what could turn out to be another disappointing year for the Boston faithful. Can you imagine that scenario today? This humility, this sense of fairness, hidden from the public, was another of Ted's heroic traits.

For the Red Sox, it was an abysmal year. The 89 losses in 154 games were the most during Yawkey's 27 years as owner. They finished in seventh place, escaping the cellar only because the Philadelphia Athletics managed to be worse. As for Ted: "I was tired a lot of the time, sore and stiff, and my neck still bothered me." On August 30, he turned 42. Another example of how long he'd been in the major leagues was the fact that he'd played in four different decades! During a game in September he hit a home run off Don Lee of the Tigers, and 20 years earlier he'd hit one off Thornton Lee, Don's father.

Joining the over-40 age set hadn't mellowed Ted as a dugout commentator. The infielder Ray Boone, like Ted a San Diego native (born five years after him), was in his last year in the major leagues in 1960. Boone once related that there was no one in the game who had as profane a vocabulary as extensive as Ted's. That season, when Ted was mad, Boone would shift himself on the bench to be closest to the walkway back to the clubhouse just to hear the hearty combination of swear words erupting from the Kid. "He could string them out without repeating a single curse word like the saltiest of sailors," Boone told me.

Overall, there wasn't much to be angry about from his own performance: Ted was having a very good season. He would bat .316, and he passed Mel Ott on the career home run list, totaling 521, which at the time put him in third place, behind only Babe Ruth's 714 and Jimmie

Foxx's 534. Ted had decided that no matter what, this would be it, and some of the ovations from fans (even in Boston!) were the loudest he had heard. (A headline of one Boston daily actually read, "What Will We Do Without Ted?") He kept demurring, though, on clubs arranging a special day for him or banquets or any goodbye event. He didn't want the pomp and the bother and people making a fuss. Plus, as Ted pointed out in his book, he found ties to be a "nuisance."

Because Ted was a big, strong man who continued to work hard at hitting, what might have gone overlooked about the Thumper as an imposing hitter into his early 40s was his mind, especially analysis and memory. David Halberstam, in *Summer of '49*, provided a particularly good explanation, comparing Ted's brain to a computer in the way that it stored memory.

There would be one more dramatic moment, the kind any ballplayer would relish, and the kind only true heroes can deliver. The last series of the season at Fenway Park was against the Orioles. Ted went to Pinky Higgins and confided he would not put his sore and tired body through the bother of a train trip to New York for the final three games. Ted did allow a ceremony before his last home game, though. He stood at home plate while testimonials were orated, gifts were given, his #9 retired; and, no doubt what Ted appreciated most, the mayor presented a $4,000 check to the Jimmy Fund. (More about that later.) But what had to be very satisfying as well was Red Sox broadcaster Curt Gowdy, emceeing the ceremony, introduced him as "the greatest hitter who ever lived."

Finally, Ted stepped to the microphone. He still didn't tip his cap, but at least he removed it. As blunt as ever, he thanked the crowd and added, "Despite some of the terrible things written about me by the knights of the keyboard up there—and they *were* terrible things, I'd like to forget them but I can't—my stay in Boston has been the most wonderful part of my life."

Attending the game was one of America's finest writers. Though most of his reputation would be built in the ensuing years, John Updike, in one of the most celebrated sports essays ever published, penned "Hub

Fans Bid Kid Adieu." It chronicled the dreary nature of the day and the inconsequential qualities of the game. However, not lost on the author was the fact that there was only one overriding reason to be in Boston. Recollecting a previous visit to Fenway Park, Updike wrote, "For me, Williams is the classic ballplayer of the game on a hot August weekday, before a small crowd, when the only thing at stake is the tissue-thin difference between a thing done well and a thing done ill."

After all that, there was that one more game to play. Updike mused, "It was for our last look that ten thousand of us had come." Ted skipped batting practice because the weather was so terrible—drizzly, dreary, wind blowing in, and the cold penetrating his 42-year-old bones. He'd have to face the side-arming lefty Steve Barber, who had not yet been born when Ted broke in with the Red Sox. But Barber lasted only four batters, walking the first three, including Ted, and was yanked in favor of Jack Fisher, a young righty. His next two times up, Ted flied out, both balls hit well but the sneering wind kept them in the park. He had one more at-bat left, in the eighth with one out. According to Updike, Ted ignored everything around him and focused on the task at hand—beating Fisher.

Today, the 78-year-old pitcher lives in Easton, Pennsylvania, around the corner from boxing champ Larry Holmes. During our conversation, Fisher proudly proclaimed that on the golf course the day before he had shot his age. When asked to come clean, had he purposely grooved a pitch to Ted that dreary afternoon, Fisher replied, "Not a chance, I was trying to win the game. I'm leading and I'm fighting for a win. There was no way that I was going to pitch around Williams. Besides, I'd had good luck against him. He doubled the first time I faced him as a rookie but had gone 0 for 11 [1-12 total] since. I didn't want my catcher to shake off the fastball. I was going with my best pitch."

(After the game upon returning to Baltimore, Fisher had the urge to call Ted, knowing he stayed in the Somerset Hotel. The operator rang the room, and he was shocked that Williams answered. "I appreciate the fact that you challenged me, gave me a chance," thanked the

Thumper. That was it. Ted hung up. "I still tell everybody he was the best I ever saw," says Fisher.)

At the plate that late afternoon, with the Fenway lights on to challenge the darkening sky, Ted took a ball, then completely whiffed on a fastball. Then Fisher tried blowing another one past Ted. But that magnificent mind and strong but weathered body had other ideas. Ted swung.

Gowdy, in the Boston broadcast booth, made the call: "Everybody quiet now here at Fenway Park after they gave him a standing ovation of two minutes knowing that this is probably his last time at bat. One out, nobody on, last of the eighth inning. Jack Fisher into his windup, here's the pitch. Williams swings—and there's a long drive to deep right! The ball is going and it is gone! A home run for Ted Williams in his last time at bat in the major leagues!"

(Years later, I worked with Curt Gowdy on the Emmy Award-winning TV show *The Way It Was.* One day he told me about his good fortune in visiting the Boston clubhouse before Ted's last game. The clubhouse guy called him over and whispered that Ted wasn't going to New York with the team for the season's final series. That they weren't packing his gear. Gowdy regaled in the fact that he had a powerful piece of information that no one else possessed. He kept it secret, saving it just in case. And so, when Ted delivered the climactic home run, Gowdy could accurately embellish his call with . . . Ted Williams in his final at bat has hit a home run. The press had wondered how Gowdy could have made such a bold, definitive call. After all, Ted still had three games left against the Yankees. Gowdy had scooped them. The "Cowboy," as he was called, had homered, as well.)

Ted circled the bases expressionless, head down "as if our praise were a storm of rain to get out of," once again not tipping his cap. Back in the dugout, he refused entreaties to take what is now dubbed a "curtain call." As Updike described it, even the other players and umpires wanted him to come out. But Ted did not comply.

I am reminded of another sterling writer, another Pulitzer Prize winner, Red Smith, who in one of his *New York Times* columns confessed why he respected the theater of sport: "Truth strangles fiction." The economy of words say so much . . . just like the efficiency of Ted's majestic swing.

When the home half ended, Ted simply grabbed his glove and trotted out to left field. Yet when Ted turned around to face home, he found that teammate Carroll Hardy had trotted behind him, with instructions to replace him. The cheers swelled again.

With that hard-won adulation he so richly deserved, Ted Williams, who many continue to believe was the greatest hitter who ever lived, and who was my baseball hero, ran off the field and into retirement.

***

It was during that first season as the play-by-play announcer for the now-California Angels, in 1969, that I finally met my baseball hero. This time, I did not just follow him from the Book-Cadillac Hotel in Detroit to Briggs Stadium, but really had the good fortune to meet him face-to-face. In 1969, Ted Williams was the first-year manager of the Washington Senators. Anaheim Stadium was the last stop on the team's initial swing around the American League. On the night the series opened, it was my turn to do the radio pregame show, and I was determined to interview my hero.

By the time the Senators arrived in Anaheim, Ted had fielded questions from all the reporters around the league. Not only was he bored at answering the same old inquiries, but he didn't think the press as a whole had gotten any friendlier in the years since he was a player. If he viewed me as just one of the "Knights of the Keyboard," my chances of getting him to do the pregame show were not good.

I needed a hook. I found it in *The Baseball Encyclopedia*. This was when I first learned about a 1940 game when the Tigers were badly beating Boston 12-1, and Joe Cronin, rather than waste another pitcher, allowed the Hoover High School alum to take the mound for a couple of innings, harking back to his days as an outstanding pitcher in San Diego. I was betting no one had asked him about his pitching "career."

Before the game, I bounced down the dugout steps for the big moment of being in direct contact with the man I had idolized since listening to the broadcast of the 1946 All-Star Game in Detroit. Ted was staring out at his players while they took batting practice. At 50, the tall and broad-shouldered Williams was still an imposing figure. No other members of the media had dared to approach him. They circled like vultures, but none mustered the courage to enter his electrical field to ask that first question. I boldly jumped right in.

"Hi, Ted, I'm Dick Enberg, the Angels' first-year announcer," I said. "I don't have to tell you how much I admire you. In fact, you were my idol growing up . . ."

He didn't even twitch. He continued to stare straight ahead with the same intense look he once trained on opposing pitchers. I was all in, so I continued my pitch.

"I have a 10-minute pregame show tonight, and I'd be delighted and honored if you'd be my guest." Then I threw him my high, hard one. "And I don't even want to talk to you about hitting. I want to talk to you about the game when you pitched against the Tigers in 1940."

Ted turned toward me, looked me in the eye, reached out his left arm, wrapped it around my neck, and in that booming John Wayne voice he barked, "COME HERE, MEAT! TURN ON THAT TAPE RECORDER!" (I was to learn that "Meat" was almost something like an endearment from Ted.)

I only had to ask him two questions. He just kept talking, remembering every detail, including the strikeout pitch he threw to Rudy York, then still with the Tigers. Ted recounted that York, who hit 33 homers and drove in 134 runs that season, "claimed I threw him a spitball." Never once did we talk about hitting. The rookie announcer was enthralled. The rookie manager was a great interview!

During the remaining 30-plus years of Ted's life, I had occasions to cross paths with him and, most important, to become a friend to a man who usually had his guard up. Each get-together was a special, if not super, experience.

But wait a moment: How was it that "the Kid," who could be as argumentative as the day is long and was never known for patience (except for at the plate, waiting for the right pitch), got to be, of all things, a *manager*? And not in Boston, but in Washington DC—the city always known as "first in war, first in peace, and last in the American League"?

Part VII

The Splendid Splinter in Winter

Some readers might think I forgot about the trade of Ted Williams for Joe DiMaggio. I didn't. I just thought I'd discuss together the two times Ted almost became a New York Yankee. Imagine if Nomar Garciappara had been traded for Derek Jeter, or Jeter had played for the Red Sox after retiring from pinstripes. A comparison to today's baseball landscape is if Bryce Harper were to be traded for Mike Trout of the Los Angeles Angels, though they play in different leagues.

The more well-known story is that prior to the 1947 season, Tom Yawkey and Dan Topping, coowner of the Yankees, were having dinner at Toots Shor's restaurant in Manhattan. This happened to be DiMaggio's favorite watering hole, but apparently he was not present that particular evening. Also, as Toots Shor's became more popular and gawkers and tourists overwhelmed the athletes and sportswriters, Yogi Berra complained, "Nobody goes there anymore, it's too crowded."

Anyway, the two owners enjoyed cocktails with their meal, and with each round an idea made more sense—a straight-up trade of DiMaggio for Williams. The Yankees would get a lefty-batting "thumper" who could take advantage of the short right-field porch at Yankee Stadium. The Red Sox fans would watch the righty-batting "Clipper" take advantage of the Green Monster in left and play along-side his brother Dominic. Supposedly, this made so much sense that Yawkey and Topping agreed to the deal.

Years later, Ted told me that the two owners had the dynamics all wrong. "Most of my home runs weren't down the line in right field," he explained. "I hit them more to right-center. In Yankee Stadium, that was a 417-foot canyon. I would have hit fewer home runs, and Joe, a line-drive hitter, would have seen some of his best drives blocked by the top of Fenway's 37-foot left-field wall. Potential homers would've become doubles or long singles. The trade would've been a bad deal for both of us."

In any case, the next morning, though hungover, Yawkey realized he'd made a bad deal because Joe DiMaggio was five years older than Ted, and thus it could be expected his career as an elite player had a shorter shelf life than that of Ted, who at the start of the 1947 season was only 28 years old. Here is where Berra comes back into the story: Yawkey phoned Topping and said he'd still do the deal if the young, untested player, "the little guy you've got in left field," was tossed in. However hungover Topping may have been, he knew that his people projected Yogi to be the next very good catcher after Bill Dickey. No dice, and the trade was cancelled.

It was right after he retired that Ted once again almost became a Yankee, and once more Dan Topping was involved. Fred Corcoran, a pioneer in representing athletes, handled Ted's business affairs. When the 1960 season was in the books—New York had lost in a memo-rable seven-game World Series to Bill Mazeroski and the Pittsburgh Pirates—he received a call from Topping, who proposed paying Ted $125,000 for even just a part-time role with the Bronx Bombers. It is interesting to contemplate how much better the 1961 Yankees would have been if their outfield consisted of an aging Ted Williams in left, and Mickey Mantle and Roger Maris in center and right. (Ironically, Ted would have shared the position with Yogi Berra, who by then had turned most of the catching duties over to Elston Howard.) However,

Ted had decided to stay retired, so Corcoran did not approach Tom Yawkey to work something out.

Ted's plans for retirement did not go far beyond being able to fish year-round, especially in the Florida Keys, where he had purchased a house. He would have more time for family, too—he married twice more, and with his third wife, Dolores Wettach, he had a son, John-Henry, and a daughter, Claudia. Ted did not necessarily expect to be involved in Major League Baseball, though that did end up happening anyway, with mixed results. He picked up some loose change and maintained his decades-long connection to the Red Sox by being a hitting instructor, but that was only during spring training. By the time the regular season began, Ted returned to fishing. Perhaps the most remarkable part of Ted's retirement years was a deeper devotion to charity work and helping children, particularly via the Jimmy Fund. He was very much his own man and could easily refuse requests to do things he had no interest in doing, but he would not say no to children in need . . . nor did he want to.

Major League Baseball did not want to let Ted Williams go. Soon after spurning the overture from Dan Topping, Ted heard from John Fetzer, an owner of the Tigers, asking if he wanted to manage the club. This Michigan farm boy would've been thrilled to have his base-ball hero serving as the skipper in Detroit, the city that had seen some of his greatest achievements, and at Ted's favorite ballpark. But Ted wasn't ready to put on a uniform again. Plus, he would never have to for financial reasons thanks to Corcoran's handling of his business affairs, which included an endorsement deal with Sears Roebuck.

In July 1966, Ted attended his Baseball Hall of Fame induction ceremony. His fellow inductee that hot afternoon in Cooperstown was Casey Stengel. The two men had enormous regard for each other, though of course they had very different experiences with the press corps. Ted spent two days in his hotel room working on a speech, and for someone who was not a public speaker, he was universally applauded for the presentation of a speech that was both heartfelt and eloquent.

Rather than use the occasion to settle old scores, Ted thanked the members of the Baseball Writers Association of America. They had not only elected him to the Hall of Fame in his first year of eligibility, but had done so with a record 282 of 302 votes, which came as a surprise to Ted. (It was something of a shoe-on-the-other-foot event, as Joe DiMaggio had not been elected until his third year of eligibility!)

Ted went on to thank mentors from his San Diego days to when he played with the Red Sox and to say that despite all the hard work, playing major league baseball "was the greatest fun I ever had." Then he offered the audience at the conclusion of his six-minute address a truly groundbreaking statement that is worth quoting in its entirety:

> Baseball gives every American boy a chance to excel. Not just to be as good as someone else, but to be better. This is the nature of man and the name of the game. I hope that some day Satchel Paige and Josh Gibson will be voted into the Hall of Fame as symbols of the great Negro players who are not here only because they weren't given the chance.

Let's put this in perspective: One of the greatest baseball players ever—and the best pure hitter ever—devotes a significant portion of his Hall of Fame induction speech to say that Cooperstown should make room for great black ballplayers who were as good as their white contemporaries but were denied baseball immortality because of the color of their skin. If there had ever been the slightest question about the fairness of Ted Williams and his appreciation of others regardless of color, this moment answered it. And you can draw a direct line between this speech, delivered by a white superstar inductee with the stature of Ted Williams, to five years later, when Satchel Paige, Class of 1971, became the first black player inducted into the Hall of Fame. As of this writing, there are 35 former Negro Leagues players and executives enshrined in Cooperstown.

If I were behind the microphone that afternoon, I would have belted it out loud and clear, "Fans, Ted Williams has hit yet another historic grand slam. Touch 'em all, indeed!"

The induction ceremony included a gift that became one of Ted's most treasured possessions. On hand was Enos Slaughter, who presented the baseball Ted had hit for a home run in the 1941 All-Star Game. The Kid could not have been more delighted.

Michael Seidel, in his book *Ted Williams: A Baseball Life*, confirms that the Slaughter gift was one of only four treasured baseballs kept by Ted in his personal collection. The others: the ball hit for a home run off Feller, now owned by Drew Brees; a ball signed by all living .400 hitters; and a ball signed by Babe Ruth. (Seidel, an Ivy League English professor, touched base with me early in his academic life. He was a freshman player on the 1962 JV baseball team that I coached at San Fernando Valley State College. Small world!)

I'd like to include another example of Ted's sense of fairness connected to the Hall of Fame: Years later, Ted actively campaigned for Shoeless Joe Jackson to be enshrined in Cooperstown. After the "Black Sox" scandal in the 1919 World Series—the Chicago White Sox took money from a gambling syndicate led by Arnold Rothstein to allow the Cincinnati Reds to win the championship—the autocratic commissioner of baseball, Kenesaw Mountain Landis, banned several players for life, including Jackson. In his 13-year career, Jackson had compiled a .356 average. (Most people don't know he played 146 games in the 1920 season, batting .382.) Jackson was never found guilty of fixing games, though. In fact, in that 1919 World Series, he hit .375, so it sure doesn't seem he tried to throw away any games.

I thought it was quite noble of Ted to take up the cause of Shoeless Joe, but at the same time I challenged him. I argued that if you are going to put Jackson in the Hall of Fame, you've got to do the same for Pete Rose, whom Commissioner Fay Vincent had banned for gambling. Ted's response: "Oh no you don't, Buddy. The penalty was banned for lifetime. Shoeless Joe has served his penalty, Rose hasn't."

Ted did not just talk the talk, he walked the walk when it came to black ballplayers. I don't mean marching in the streets, but personal, open gestures and acts of support for the black player, throughout his career and lifetime. A few years after Ted retired as a player, when he was living full-time in Florida, during spring training he encountered a young pitcher with the Athletics, John "Blue Moon" Odom. Though the hotel where the Oakland players were staying was no longer a legally whites-only establishment, the front desk had turned Odom away. Observing this and after a brief conversation with the dejected young man, Ted took Odom back to the registration desk. Magically, a room became available.

From what was written earlier, we already know that Ted was the skipper of the Washington Senators. But facing a comfortable retirement of hunting and fishing and living full-time in Florida, why would he take on such a tough job? The answer: Bob Short. He was the new owner of the capital's club, and he got it into his head that Ted would be a good manager . . . the same Ted Williams who once proclaimed, "All managers are losers, they are the most expendable pieces of furniture on the face of the Earth."

In the early 1960s, former batting champ Mickey Vernon had suffered two years at the helm of the team—losing 100 and 101 games, respectively—then was gone after 40 games of a third season, replaced by Eddie Yost. As a player, Yost, renowned for his mastery of the strike zone, earned the nickname the "Walking Man." The moniker fit his experience in his role with the Senators. He managed a total of one game—a loss, naturally—and was told to take a hike. He in turn was replaced by Gil Hodges, who had retired as a player in 1963 as a member of the New York Mets, managed by Stengel. The best Hodges could do was finish nine games under .500 in 1967, then he returned to the Mets, as the skipper. Jim Lemon managed the club the next year, and that is when Short launched his campaign to coax Ted back into the dugout.

While I was resisting the offer to do the Angels play-by-play, Ted was balking at the offer from Short. Why give up the fishing, self-imposed schedule, and time with John-Henry and Claudia? It boiled down to the man who could so easily say no but could not say no to Bob Short, whom Ted admired for his intelligence. Among the incentives was Ted would receive an option to purchase 10 percent of the franchise as well as a five-year contract.

All this proved irresistible. When the 1969 season began, Ted Williams was the manager of the Washington Senators. (The slugger Frank Howard already wore no. 9, but he gave it up out of respect for his new skipper.) One result, it should be pointed out, was Ted invented the role of "bench coach," a common practice in major league dugouts today. The rookie manager realized that at least until he gained some experience, he could use another set of eyes and ears during games. He tried to entice Johnny Pesky for the job, but when Needle, by then a Red Sox coach, said no, Ted hired Joe Comacho, a good friend who was the director of the summer camps Ted hosted for youngsters.

To the surprise of some people, especially those in the press box, the team finally had a winning record. Picked to finish in last place (as usual), the Senators compiled an 86-76 record and earned fourth place in the American League with pretty much the same roster as the previous year, when the team won just 65 games. It was the franchise's first winning season in 17 years. No doubt thanks to having the greatest hitter of all time as manager, the team batting average leaped from .224 in the 1968 season to .251. Howard had a career-high 48 home runs and double his total of walks. The light-hitting shortstop Ed Brinkman's batting average went from .187 to .266. The pitching, too, improved, with the team ERA going from 3.64 to 3.49. Also making a big impression was the record-breaking attendance of 918,000 fans in 1969, nearly double the 546,661 who saw Washington play the year before.

Ted became the first-ever player voted Most Valuable Player to earn Manager of the Year honors. When he was informed of the award, it was typical Ted: "I'm terribly disappointed that Billy Martin [Twins] and Earl Weaver [Orioles] didn't get it. Both of them did a helluva job and both of them deserved the honor."

The following year, Ted took his second turn as an author, having published *My Turn at Bat* in 1969. Ted's *The Science of Hitting* has

served as a treasured batting bible for nearly 50 years. Published in
1970, its influence continues to be significant among baseball's best
hitters today. Kris Bryant, Joey Votto, Bryce Harper, Daniel Murphy,
and Josh Donaldson are among baseball's elite batters to acknowledge being strong supporters of Ted's hitting theories.

Bryant, the Cubs' 2015 National League Rookie of the Year and
2016 National League MVP, is powerful evidence that you needn't
be a left-handed hitter to move to the head of the class. You just have
to execute what Ted taught. His father, Mike, a Red Sox minor league
outfielder for two years (1981-82) and now a full-time hitting instructor in Las Vegas, sat at the feet of the Master and totally subscribes to
Ted's science of hitting. "I articulate what I value, what works, but
I always give all the credit to Ted," Mike told me. "I marvel at his
simplicity, but it was so advanced. What worked 60 years ago, works
today. Nothing else makes sense. All the more remarkable was Ted
was self-taught. No video, no batting instructors, no cybermetrics,
but he figured it out . . . and it's still relevant: simply get the pitch on
a downward plane and hit it squarely with an upward swing . . . start
below the shoulders and finish above the shoulders . . . get the front
elbow above your shoulders as soon as you can . . . hit it hard and hit it
in the air, the core of his philosophy. And of course, get a good pitch
to hit."

Mike Bryant is grateful for being in the right place at the right time.
He grew up in Acton, a half-hour west of Boston, as a Red Sox and
Williams fan. He was drafted as an outfielder by Boston in the ninth
round. In the minor league camp in spring training, Williams, as the
roving instructor, would offer bonus advise to anyone who wanted to
be on the field ready to hit by 6 in the morning. "I couldn't wait, got
there at 5:45 and he still yelled that I was friggin' late, another baseball and life lesson. I listened to his three-hour lectures, mesmerized,
never saying a word, for two weeks. At age 14 my parents had given
me *The Science of Hitting*, but you really needed someone to teach it.
And here I was one-to-one, a pupil in the classroom with the greatest

hitter ever. Those precious sessions are the basis of what I taught Kris and what I teach my students today."

After a surprisingly successful season, could Ted school the Washington Senators to reach for even greater heights—like possibly contend for the pennant the next season? Alas, no. The team could only collect 70 victories, and the 92 losses included a 14-game losing streak. The 1971 season was even worse, with a 63-96 record, finishing 38.5 games out of first place. Bob Short moved the franchise west from Washington, and they became the Texas Rangers. A different location, name, and uniform did not improve a team with little talent and players who had stopped listening to their manager. After a 54-100 finish, Ted stepped down.

It was time to return to being a full-time fisherman.

***

Through time, good and bad, there was plenty of evidence for me to build in my admiration for Ted. On one hand, he didn't hide his personal dislikes—you knew where you stood with him. How often did I hear him as a manager say that he hated all pitchers, even his own, a hangover from his playing days? On the other hand, he was faithful in words and action to those he cared about and trusted. If he liked someone, he was unfailingly true to that relationship . . . to the very end.

You can learn a lot about a hero based on how he acts around other stars and public figures. Dominic DiMaggio experienced that firsthand. To the last of his days—which ended in 2009, at age 92—Dominic professed his love for his brother Joe. However, in their later years, it was Ted who was more of a brother to Dominic.

When he was up north, Ted was a regular and most welcome visitor at the DiMaggio home in Marion, Massachusetts. (They would see one another in Florida, too, after Dominic and Emily bought a house in Palm Beach.) Ted adored Dominic's beautiful wife and her warm, vibrant personality. For many years, he called her "the Queen" and seemingly could never refuse a request. Ted was treated like a member of the family.

"My favorite memory of Ted was a dinner we had at Mom and Dad's Massachusetts house," recalls Dominic DiMaggio Jr. "We were all sitting at the dining room table and Ted had his back to the fireplace and was telling the story about his being shot down in the Korean War. He was sitting on one of the delicate antique spindle chairs at the table and he was incredibly energetic in his storytelling.

"He was at the climax of the story when he was communicating with his wing man while taking direct fire from behind and he made a gesture in the direction of where he was going to make an evasive move. He was such a big guy and was so engaged in his story that he spun his left arm and body in the direction of his move and snapped the entire back off the antique chair. He immediately lost all his vigor, stopping the story. After the chair snapped, there was dead silence at the table quickly followed by gales of laughter from the family, with Ted left totally embarrassed and apologizing to Mom like a teenager who just screwed up. I am sure he eventually finished the story, but we all felt so bad for him that I don't remember the outcome, except he, obviously, made it back alive.

"My second favorite story: I had never realized how imposing a father and authority figure Ted could be, as we always saw him as a jovial friend of Dad's, until one night when Ted's son, John-Henry, and I went out in Marion to make the rounds of the local bars. John-Henry was in college at Bates in Maine and he was of legal drinking age, and so was I of course. We arrived home smelling like a bar and pretty woozy, so we went to watch TV and found Ted sitting in the den, apparently waiting up for us. It had not occurred to me that at majority age any of our parents would be awaiting our return—but Ted was and he wasn't happy. His first comment to John-Henry was, 'Were you smoking?!? You stink!' At that point I immediately turned around and headed for the kitchen to raid the ice box and avoid the coming storm. From the safety of the kitchen I could hear John-Henry being dressed down by his dad, and boy, I was glad to be in a different room! When it was all over John-Henry joined me in the kitchen, a lot more sober than just ten minutes before. We commiserated about parents and went to bed. I had gained a new respect for Mr. Williams and maybe a little animosity, but today I realize he was just being a good father, trying to guide his son down the correct path.

"To me, Ted was a great guy, a man's man, and the real-life version of the acting persona of John Wayne."

To me, another definition of a hero is someone who is loyal to his friends. Ted was surely that, especially to his old Red Sox buddies. Just one example involves Dominic Jr.'s father: assisted by Bill Gilbert, Dominic Sr. wrote a book, *Real Grass, Real Heroes: Baseball's Historic 1941 Season*, which was published in April 1990 by Zebra, a subsidiary of Kensington Books.

Ted, not Joe, contributed the introduction, and it was a pretty humble one coming from the last ballplayer to break the .400 barrier. "Asking me to write about the 1941 baseball season is doing me a favor, especially for a book by my friend Dom DiMaggio," Ted began. He added: "I don't take a backseat to anybody in my respect and fondness for Dom. There is no finer person on earth."

When the opportunity arose, Ted's actions backed up his words—Dominic and the publisher planned a book-launch party at the toney Tavern On the Green restaurant on the edge of Central Park in Manhattan. With Joe living nearby, many people, including the publisher, expected that he would attend, even if for only a few minutes to congratulate his brother and get a free copy. But Joe didn't show. Ted did—making the trip up from Florida, unannounced. That night, they were brothers from different mothers as Ted hugged "Dommie" and praised his former teammate.

There is a footnote to this story that further emphasizes Ted's loyalty to teammates, from fellow stars to those struggling to stay in the big show. As David Halberstam tells it, Zebra Books had arranged a dinner for Dominic and a few friends at the 21 Club after the party. Ted, of course, was invited to go along. But he explained that Jerry

Casale, who had won 13 games as a Beantown rookie pitcher in 1958, had just opened his own restaurant, Pino's, on 34th Street. In a phone call, Casale had mentioned that it sure would mean a lot for business if Ted Williams ate there, and the Kid had promised he would. But he didn't want to leave Dominic flat. Wisdom won out—everyone decided to go to Pino's for dinner instead. Less than an hour later, Casale was doing a great business.

Ted's incomparable baseball career and his unwavering loyalty to friends plus his serious support of black players is the right stuff of a real hero. Add what he did for others, most of them strangers, and most of them children, and I admire him all the more. Those who don't know about this side of him are not seeing the true Ted Williams, especially his big heart.

A major Boston and New England charity is the Jimmy Fund, founded in 1948 (a year in which Ted hit .369) to support the tremendous work done by the Dana Farber Institute, which conducts cancer research and provides treatment to children. From the very start, Ted went deep, very active in supporting events that raised funds for the institute. (The cover photo of this book was taken while I was in Boston broadcasting a 1976 Angels series against the Red Sox and Ted was in town for a Jimmy Fund function.) In fact, mention Jimmy Fund and the first name that comes to mind is Ted Williams— a tribute to his sincere, inspirational, and generous involvement. It is no coincidence that during the years 1948 to 2000, when Ted had become physically unable to do fundraising, the Jimmy Fund raised over half a billion dollars.

When asked about Ted's efforts, a spokesperson for the Jimmy Fund stated, "Ted Williams would travel everywhere and anywhere, no strings or paychecks attached, to support the cause. His name is synonymous with our battle against all forms of cancer."

Late in the summer of 1953, soon after Ted returned from Korea, the Red Sox wanted to stage a welcome home event. Normally, he would have shunned the attention. But when it was suggested that the event could be a $100-a-plate dinner for the Jimmy Fund, Ted gave his blessing. The dinner was held at the Hotel Statler and was attended by baseball and Red Sox officials, Ted's teammates, celebrities like Ed Sullivan, and about one thousand people. The event itself raised over $100,000 for the Jimmy Fund, plus a $50,000 check was donated by the Joseph Kennedy family, which was presented by Ted Kennedy, then 21 years old.

Year after year, continuing as an active player and then especially during his retirement years, Ted attended dinners and participated in other big and small fundraising activities. The opportunity to meet Ted Williams was a big reason why events were well-attended and wallets were opened wide. Also big supporters and fundraisers for the Jimmy Fund were Dominic and Emily DiMaggio. The latter remembers, "There were times I had organized an event and for whatever reason ticket sales were not going well. When I got really stuck, I called Ted down in Florida. I didn't want to bother him and I was all apologies, but all Ted would say is, 'When do you need me there?' If time was tight, Ted was on the next plane. He was lovely to everybody, we'd fill the charity coffers, and with a smile and a wave Ted was on his way back to fishing."

In his book *Ted Williams: The Biography of An American Hero*, Leigh Montville describes "A Night With Ted Williams," a major charity event held in November 1988. It raised well over a quarter million dollars with Ted as the featured honoree that year. While Ted relished his vocal dissertations on hitting, he never boasted of his support of many charities, but especially the Jimmy Fund. "The quickest way to get Williams to stop talking," wrote Montville, "was to ask him about his charity work. This was personal, private, no cameras or attention allowed. He would go public, help raise enough money to keep the Jimmy Fund alive, vibrant, all by himself, but the visits to kids were almost always done in secrecy."

Harold Kaese, one of the more prominent Boston sportswriters, broke the "embargo" once by informing readers about a local car mechanic who discovered that Ted had paid his child's hospital bill—and this was a guy who used to go to Fenway Park to razz the left fielder. Another reporter wrote that Ted not only showed up to engage the sick youngsters in conversation, but he arrived bearing gifts like toys and even TV sets, paid for out of his own pocket.

As those two reporters indicated, as strong as Ted's support of the Jimmy Fund and other established charities were, his one-on-one visits to children with life-threatening illnesses far outnumbered big-ticket events. (This was all in addition to his consistent support of his mother, father, and brother for the rest of their lives.) His kindness and caring came straight from the depth of his soul.

Countless times, Ted visited sick children in their homes and in hospital rooms. The stories, not reported at the times they took place, are astonishing in their frequency. In May 1947, he visited a boy in the hospital who was a double amputee and promised a homer in his next game if the kid would find a way to get up and walk—Ted hit two, both over the Green Monster in left. Two seasons later, he dedicated a home run to a 14-year-old polio victim and delivered. The terrific biographies by Montville and Bradlee Jr. are replete with such incidents.

Mike Andrews, a former Boston second baseman who served as the executive director and chairman of the Jimmy Fund for over 30 years, confirmed to me the touching incident related by Montville: "Like the kid who was dying and wouldn't let go of Ted's finger. Ted just pulled a cot next to him and slept there all night, the kid holding Ted's finger. The way Ted got to know kids was remarkable, he came back to see them, again and again always remembered their names. He'd show up anytime."

No wonder I wanted to be Ted Williams!

Ted would bring dozens of baseballs to the hospital to sign for the kids.

He had a clever ploy for raising money for charity. He'd endorse any check for more than $1. That way the donor had the Thumper's autograph. Purportedly, that worked later in another scheme. He would pay for dinners with a personal check. It was like getting a free meal, because the restaurateur would never cash such a prized souvenir autograph. Smart.

On several occasions, and before travel became trying with age, Ted even chartered planes to visit children. Nevertheless, he didn't stop on behalf of the Jimmy Fund and the secret visits to ill children and their awestruck, grateful families. The former Red Sox president Larry Lucchino told me that the legacy of Ted Williams continues. At present, the Jimmy Find generates $80 million annually in charitable gifts. Oh my!

***

That baseball is my favorite sport partly explains why I enjoyed broadcasting Angels games. Certainly, this wasn't because the franchise was successful—one indication of futility was the team had eight managers from 1969 to 1978! Having Don Drysdale as a partner in the booth from 1973 compensated for the many disappointing seasons. He made baseball broadcasting fun, refusing to let me rue and stew over the many losses. "Don't take it so seriously," he'd say after yet another beating. "If they don't give a crap, why should you? Let's go, I'll buy you a drink."

Among Don's many valuable qualities is he knew the game inside and out. His Hall of Fame résumé as a player all those years with the Brooklyn and Los Angeles Dodgers (until an arm injury forced him to retire at only 33) includes 209 victories, a 2.95 career ERA, and in 1968 he threw six shutouts in a row on the way to a then-major league record 58 consecutive scoreless innings. Deservedly, Bob Gibson's 1.12 ERA in 1968 received most of the attention, but that year Drysdale was virtually unhittable, too. If I had ever owned a major league franchise, my first move would have been to hire Drysdale as my manager. He would have been a fabulous skipper. He knew pitching (obviously!), he knew how to have fun, and he would have been tough when he needed to be tough. I've always felt there should be a side to an effective manager that could strike fear in a player. The big right-hander had that quality. Ask any hitter who crowded the plate on him.

Another valuable quality was a wonderful sense of humor to complement that ability to have fun. We had a great relationship away from the ballpark and an even better one in the broadcast booth. We developed an open-mike system so that both of us could talk in the same inning. As the lead announcer, I called six innings and Don worked three, but we had microphone toggle switches that allowed each of us to go on the air whenever we wanted. We knew that going one-on-one we'd never beat Vin Scully, the broadcasting poet of the Dodgers, but we thought the two of us together would be reasonably competitive for the Southern California audience.

It was during my tenure with the Angels that I saw the most dominant game I've ever seen pitched: Nolan Ryan's 6-0 no-hitter against the Tigers in 1973. In the first seven innings, he was absolutely overpowering, striking out 16 batters with 100-mile-an-hour fastballs and hellacious curves. The broadcast booth that hung off the facing of the second deck in Detroit—my old haunt (and Ted's), Briggs Stadium, had been replaced in name by Tigers Stadium—was close enough to the field that you could hear the velocity of his pitches as they sung their defiant message into the catcher's glove, complemented by his lusty grunts as he delivered the high hard ones. With two outs in the ninth inning, first baseman Norm Cash, a former American League batting champion who had already struck out twice, stepped up to the plate holding a piano leg instead of a bat. After taking strike one, the umpire, Ron Luciano, sent Cash back to the dugout for a bat. Cash laughed and said, "What the hell difference does it make? I'm not going to hit him anyway." Sure enough, he popped up, and Ryan had his second no-hitter of the season.

This game offered plenty of opportunities for me to employ two expressions that had become part of my repertoire: "Oh my!" and "Touch 'em all!" A third, "The halo shines tonight," was reserved for home wins at the "Big A" stadium in Anaheim. On that July day, the halo certainly hovered over Nolan Ryan's cap, that's for certain.

I often wondered while covering Ryan's incredible dominance how he would have fared against Ted. I do believe the Thumper would have held his own. No question Ryan, whose control wasn't always the best, would have walked him a lot. But a 100-mile-an-hour fastball over the plate to Ted? That would have been like hanging a steak over the head of a Doberman pinscher.

As much as I did love doing those Angels games and thought the world of Gene Autry, my broadcasting career continued to expand beyond baseball. These experiences were some of the most memorable moments in my life, and for many sports fans, too.

In the 1970s, I began a 25-year relationship with NBC Sports. During that time, the network sent me everywhere except Antarctica to call college and NBA basketball, boxing, college and pro football, figure skating, golf, gymnastics, horse racing, tennis, track and field, and the Olympics in addition to baseball. After the first two years, I did have to relinquish broadcasting Angels games, because, reluctantly, I had to admit I couldn't do everything. Still, it was a busy, fulfilling, and rewarding quarter-century—and I was far from done with baseball. One of the favorite roles was anchoring a college basketball game of the week package, with my "wing men," two very special color commentators, Billy Packer and Al McGuire.

If you'll indulge me, I'd like to share several of those great sports experiences. One has to be when Michigan State played Indiana State for the NCAA Championship in March 1979 in Salt Lake City. The anticipation of this showdown as the two schools defeated all the other competition truly was the beginning of what we know as March Madness. The Spartans, coached by Judd Heathcote and inspired by Magic Johnson, and the Sycamores, led by Larry Bird, met. The more remarkable story was that of the "Cinderella," Indiana State, because the mid-major school had not even been ranked in preseason polls. Bird was the only starter from the previous season to return, and as the season was about to begin, their coach, Bob King, had a heart attack. He retired and was replaced by Bill Hodges. Yet, entering the championship game, Indiana State was a perfect 33-0. Michigan State was 25-6 but riding a hot streak led by their charismatic sophomore.

I was at courtside that night with Al and Billy. The halftime show was hosted by Bryant Gumbel. We anticipated a very good audience—and as it turned out, the Nielsen rating for that game was higher than any previous basketball game in the US, estimated at 40 million viewers. The TV "audience share" (percentage of sets in use) is still a record. The Spartans won by 11 points. The popularity of the game greatly increased the interest in college basketball. And with both Magic and Bird going into the pros the following season, that 1979 NCAA championship game was a preview of the intense rivalry between the Lakers and Celtics through the 1980s.

I've long enjoyed thoroughbred racing and have even owned a few horses. This apple picker learned the hard way why they call it the "sport of kings." As the well-worn saying goes, "The best way to make a million dollars in horse racing is to start out with $5 million." Anyway, I've seen and broadcast hundreds of horse races, so it might seem odd that the most memorable for me was a Breeder's Cup event, in November 1984. I was the NBC host of that very first Breeder's Cup, at the fabled Hollywood Park racetrack. It was dubbed "Racing's Greatest Day" because of the seven races for an unprecedented $10 million in purses, including the $3 million Breeder's Cup Classic. One of my roles was to interview Hollywood celebrities, including Fred Astaire, Elizabeth Taylor, John Forsythe, and Tim Conway. As we were pressed tightly in NBC's makeshift booth, I had a close-up look at Ms. Taylor's beauty, and yes, her eyes were a stunning violet. She was very nervous, almost shaking. It took great resolve on my part not to give her a comforting hug.

Back to the races: Competing wire-to-wire toward an amazing finish were Preakness winner Gate Dancer, the favorite Slew o' Gold, and longshot Wild Again, clearly not the favorite at 31-1 odds. Every second of that race was more thrilling than the last, and with the 68,000 on hand, I had to wait 10 minutes after the three horses crossed the finish line to learn that Wild Again had survived an inquiry and was the winner. Oh my! Now, that was a big-money horse race! A $2 bet on the winner paid $64.

In 1999, the Ryder Cup was at The Country Club in Brookline, Massachusetts, where 86 years earlier the local amateur Francis Ouimet had defeated Harry Vardon and Ted Ray in the US Open and put golf on the front page of American newspapers. The European players were ascendant in the Ryder Cup, and, led by Seve Ballesteros, they had won in 1997. It looked like more of the same after the first two days of the international event, with Europe accumulating a 10-6 lead and needing only 4 points in Sunday's 12 singles matches to retain the Cup. But the captain, Ben Crenshaw, promised victory, and on that Sunday Tiger Woods, Phil Mickelson, Davis Love III, Justin Leonard (with that breathtaking 45-foot putt on 17), Payne Stewart (who would die in a plane crash a month later), and the other Americans delivered. It remains the greatest win in Ryder Cup history.

In 1973, I was part of a six-man TV crew allowed into what was then Peking (now Beijing) to broadcast the first-ever basketball game between teams representing the United States and the People's Republic of China. The invitation was from Zhou Enlai (as his name is now spelled), second only to Mao. His wife, Madam Mao, rarely seen in public, greeted us at the game. This event came less than a year after President Nixon's groundbreaking trip to China, and other than a handful of ping-pong matches, it was the first official competition of any sport between the two nations. Among the young American players involved were George Karl of the University of North Carolina (now an NBA coach), Lon Kruger of Kansas State, Rich Kelley of Stanford, Quinn Buckner of Indiana, and Kevin Grevey of Kentucky. The US won handily in what was a mind-bending experience. My opening to the broadcast was done in an empty Tiananmen Square, and my closing was on the Great Wall. Oh my!

In other international events, there is nothing like covering the Wimbledon tennis championships. My most memorable was 1979 because it was the first-ever live broadcast of the event. This was before the Indianapolis 500 and the Olympics and the NBA Finals were shown live. On that Saturday at 9 a.m. (Eastern time), NBC had to preempt such shows as "Daffy Duck" and "Godzilla Super 90," and some kids weren't the least bit happy. It had been a great tournament, with players like Björn Borg, Jimmy Connors, John McEnroe, Chris Evert, and Martina Navratilova at or nearing their primes. In the men's final we had Borg, the three-time defending champion, against the power-serving American lefty Roscoe Tanner, after Navratilova had defeated Evert in the women's final the day before. Borg won his eighth major in five stirring sets to capture his fourth Wimbledon in a row, and our live broadcast helped tennis to explode internationally— though not without some incredible behind-the-scenes maneuvering to assure that first-ever live telecast of Wimbledon began on time to assure a proper NBC opening.

Most of us at the 1972 Olympics in Munich were excited to be at the epicenter of international sports those two and a half weeks, but none of us expected to be in the middle of international terrorism. The competitions were enormously thrilling, with highlights including Mark Spitz's record-setting seven gold medals (being Jewish, he was asked to leave Munich early because of the terrorist attack), the coronation of Olga Korbut as a queen of gymnastics, the US men's basketball team's controversial loss to the Soviet Union and refusing to accept the silver medal, Lasse Viren winning the rare double in the 5,000 and 10,000 meters, and at only age 15, the Australian swimmer Shane Gould earning three gold medals and a silver and a bronze.

But of course most memorable about the Munich games was the attack that took the lives of 11 Israeli athletes and coaches, and in the ensuing gun battle five Black September Palestinian terrorists were killed. It was a terrible blow to the Germans, who had meticulously planned for their return as Olympics hosts. From the brilliant architecture of the main stadium to the warm welcome to the world, this was Germany's opportunity to erase the events of Hitler's 1936 Berlin Games, and all was orchestrated perfectly until that fateful night.

Unaware of what had transpired, I arrived early the next morning by car from my Bavarian hotel, one hour south of Munich, to find the streets leading to the Olympic complex lined with armored vehicles. Soon I would learn of the tragedy. Even with the attack, I was able with a simple press credential to advance within a couple hundred yards of the site. Clearly, the world was not prepared for this first act of public terror. And of course, all of our hearts sank when we heard that all those Israeli Olympians were gone.

Let me return to my most cherished of all sports, and my baseball idol. That pregame interview I did with Ted Williams at Anaheim Stadium in 1969 was an ice-breaker and the beginning of a friendship that would last for three decades.

For the first 10 years or so after our initial encounter, whenever I met Ted—as a manager, at a charitable function, or as a guest on my TV show *Sports Challenge*—he always remembered me. If he saw me in a group of people, he'd call me over, bellowing, "HEY, MEAT, HOW'S IT GOING?" I got interviews nobody else did. The press always walked on eggs around Ted, and I considered it a special honor to receive his acknowledgment. To me, Ted was always charming, bold, smart, fascinating, and warm. I am fully aware that many people aren't as fortunate and don't get the same reaction when meeting their heroes.

I wish we had seen each other more during the rest of the 1970s and into the '80s. Ted was content to spend almost all of his time fishing and otherwise living his life in Florida, except for business obligations and especially charity-related travels. For an article for *Esquire* magazine in 1986, Richard Ben Cramer (who would later write a popular biography of Joe DiMaggio) visited Ted at his home in Islamorada on the Florida Keys.

"He is a hard man to meet," Cramer wrote about Ted. "This is not to paint him as a hermit or a shrinking flower, Garbo with a baseball bat. No, in his home town, Ted is hard not to *see*. He's out every day, out early and loud."

I was smack-dab in the middle of the whirlwind that was my career. But when we did cross paths, Ted was always mesmerizing to be around. He was so passionate about his two main loves, hitting a baseball and fishing. With both subjects, he was very opinionated—and deservedly so! When he spoke, you were on the edge of your seat.

Thankfully, during the last 15 years of Ted's life, we saw each other more often. One reason was he visited his birthplace of San Diego more frequently, and I had moved there with Barbara and our family. With age, Ted mellowed wonderfully. He became softer and friendlier and reached out to people. He was reinforced by the personal contact. And people liked him. When we'd walk into a restaurant or hotel, and strangers would greet him, he'd never brush them off. Ted would not only shake their hands, he would stop and talk. In fact, he would try to draw them out.

Just one example was when I was invited to join Bob Breitbard for breakfast at Amber's Restaurant in a Holiday Inn off Highway 15 in San Diego. Bob had been Ted's best friend at Hoover High and was the founder and executive director of the San Diego Hall of Champions. Ted came charging through the front door like a fullback with his big voice roaring, "*I* know the toughest sport to broadcast."

While not phrased as a question, it was meant for me. His way was to ask a lot of questions, and most often he already knew the answer—he just wanted to see if you did. Well, I got him, this time.

"What's your answer, Ted?"

"Basketball."

"Not a chance. The game is fast. Only 10 guys on the court, all easily identifiable. The action carries the announcer."

Back bellows the Thumper, still not taking a seat: "Okay, what is the toughest?"

"It's your game, baseball." I explained how the rhythms of the game, the slower action challenged the man calling the play-by-play to fill delays with interesting material, while at the same time always being primed to be on top of an exciting moment. He never liked being wrong, even in this simple exchange, but the fact that the answer was baseball left him pleased enough.

While Ted's reputation for being cold and cantankerous was sometimes deserved, he had mellowed a lot by this late stage of his life. It was interesting to see him politely and sincerely engage the waiter and others around us. He asked personal questions. "People treat me so damn good," he explained to Bob and me, "I got to take time to show I appreciate it. Now and then I get a wise guy, but I know how to cool them off." Right!

***

It was in 1991 that Ted cooled off—or should I say warmed up—to the Fenway fans, and a mutual admiration developed between them. In May, the Red Sox staged a Ted Williams Day. By this point, Ted had his fill of being the center of attention anywhere, but this was indeed special, a celebration of the 50th anniversary of the last time a major league player batted over .400. The cheers from the crowd touched that big heart, and Ted finally did what no one thought they would ever see again: Ted tipped his cap to the Boston fans.

There was another honor, that August. Ted and Joe DiMaggio were invited to the White House to receive the Presidential Medal of Freedom from President George H. W. Bush, a big baseball fan (he had played first base on the Yale University team) and a decorated World War II combat pilot. The chief of staff who orchestrated the ceremony was John Sununu, who had been a three-term governor of New Hampshire and also an avid baseball fan. (Apparently, voters in the Granite State did not hold it against him that the Yankees were his team.) He recently told me, "Ted Williams was a great patriot and war hero who happened to be a great baseball hero." Ted's regard for the president was such that he actually wore a tie— no easy feat for the Kid. He couldn't wait to take it off, and when he did, he autographed it and gave it to Sununu, a unique prize indeed.

About the entire experience, Sununu laughed and said, "I was so impressed by Ted that I decided to take it easier on my eight kids, all Red Sox fans."

In February 1994, the Ted Williams Museum opened in Citrus Hills, Florida. It was the first ever such tribute to a living athlete. The gala opening attracted a bevy of sports stars, including Joe DiMaggio, Bobby Orr, Dominic DiMaggio, and Muhammad Ali. Ted loved Ali, and the former heavyweight champ loved Ted. So much so, that Ali arrived several days before the opening and conducted several interviews to promote the event. He also stayed well after the gala was over, signing hundreds of autographs.

Later, Ali and his personal photographer and friend, Howard Bingham, had dinner with Ted, which lasted over three hours. While Ali was there, he read Ted's Cooperstown induction speech and cried when he read the part where Williams campaigned for the inclusion in the Hall of Fame of the great Negro League players. Even "The Greatest" was deeply moved by Ted's fairness and integrity.

This event reminded me of sitting on the dais next to the boxing champion at an American Sportscasters Association dinner in New York City two years earlier, when Ali was honored as the Sports Legend of the Year. Nearly 1,000 attended. Throughout the evening, the line from the dinner audience to Ali snaked yards into the ballroom. I offered my services to stop the flow of autograph seekers, since he had no time to enjoy his meal. Ali strongly rejected my offer, saying, "I'll sign every one." And he did. The dinner program was delayed almost an hour.

Even though in 1996 I was fully engaged with major NBC Sports assignments that provided a steady diet of NFL football, NCAA basketball, Wimbledon, and PGA golf, my heart still pulsated with the rhythms of baseball. It was no secret in San Diego that Ted was my idol. The owner of the Padres at that time, John Moores, was kind enough to invite me and my wife to his home for a private celebration with Ted. It was a brilliant 80-degree day in the beginning of February. Since the weather was like midsummer, how appropriate that baseball commanded my evening. The party in their impressive Rancho Santa Fe home was to salute Ted, who was in town for the 50th anniversary of the San Diego Hall of Champions dinner.

The guest of honor was then 77. Despite a couple of debilitating strokes, he was still imposing. And age could not mask his powerfully handsome face. While he wobbled when standing without a cane's support, he stood "big." His shoulders were not slumped, but square. The years had not shrunken him, just as the opposing pitchers a half-century ago could not reduce him to mortal size. He was still the biggest man at the party. "And not as tough and as bitter as I thought," reflected my wife, Barbara, who was meeting him for the first time. Oh, he *was* tough, I assured her, but yes, he had mellowed.

After dinner, he sat on a large padded couch in the Mooreses' living room. The other guests, some 20 couples, surrounded the San Diego legend as Bob Breitbard announced the formation of an endowment program in Ted's name. From my position directly across the room from Ted, I could view a wall of portraits behind him, four large black-and-white photographs of the Mooreses' historical heroes, admired leaders. In the upper left: Winston Churchill. Upper right: Muhammad Ali. Lower left: Georgia O'Keeffe. Lower right: Ernest Hemingway. They covered a large expanse of the wall just above Ted's head. The fifth hero was seated in living color directly between and below O'Keefe and Hemingway—Ted Williams, San Diego's Splendid Splinter, Teddy Ballgame. He was thanking Breitbard and our hosts. And then to the rest of us, he simply expressed his respect for anyone who had made him feel back at home in San Diego. It looked as if Hemingway were smiling over this remarkable scene, a five-person gallery of greatness.

Ted spoke briefly, reluctantly, of his five military years of flying, two of them spent in combat in Korea piloting fighter jets, where he crashed and walked away. He also mentioned casually that he won the Triple Crown three times (once in Minneapolis and twice in Boston). At one point he wiped tears from his eyes, the tears brought by failing eyes, and eyes fatigued by a demanding day that began in Florida eighteen hours earlier. I fought back my own, but mine were tears of joy. I was allowed to be an adoring kid again. My idol was in the same room. And he recognized me in front of those gathered. What a night! Everything was complete except for one small detail. I wish he'd called me "Meat" just one more time.

Let me just add that before the Rancho Santa Fe dinner, Colonel Jerry Coleman was interviewing Williams for the Padres radio-TV broadcast. John Moores said that he eased close by to hear the conversation and heard Jerry ask, "Don't you regret missing five seasons due to the military service?" Ted replied, "No, how could I? I came back alive." As Moores related the incident, I had a lump in my throat. Coleman, the ex-Yankee and the only major leaguer to fly fighter planes in two separate wars and amazingly survive 120 combat missions, was asking the questions of a man who lived through 39 missions in Korea, once surviving a spectacular jet crash landing. Both were American heroes. About his own military heroes, Ted once told me, "Their greatness was *beyond the reach*. It's just overwhelming what they could do. Hard to imagine how they did it."

The Hall of Champions dinner was a few days later, and it attracted a record audience of 1,200. The overflow crowd was testimony to this being a significant milestone, to those being honored . . . and Ted Williams would be present. They paid a generous warm tribute to Hall of Fame inductees Randy Jones, a Cy Young winner with the Padres, and PGA Tour champion Craig Stadler, as well as the amateur and professional San Diego sports stars of 1995, George Jones and Tony Gwynn. And there were special honorees, such as Rick Draney (wheelchair basketball), Buzzie Bavasi (community), and Hall of Champions founder Bob Breitbard. I was privileged to be the emcee.

Ted looked exhausted. It had been a tough week, answering demands from every corner—taping a TV special, interviewing for newspaper columnists and TV sportscasters, and answering requests from his many fans, including the Mooreses. Each wanted a memorable piece of him—a photo, a word, a handshake, an autograph, a look. My role placed me in a delicate spot. It was obvious upon first glance that this would be a wonderful night, but a *long* night. In fact, early in the evening, Ted's son, John-Henry, came to my seat on the dais and asked if there was *any* chance we could alter the schedule to put Ted's award at the beginning of the program so that he might have an early exit. I wanted to say yes, but the prepared video sequence would have been destroyed, and more important, the climactic drama of the evening would have been lost. Ted Williams had to hit clean-up.

Finally, to his third standing ovation of the night, Ted, helped by John-Henry, made it to the podium. He lost his balance and staggered as he reached the microphone. I wondered if some in the audience, unaware of his paralysis, might have thought he had been overserved. How unfair, and yet there was no way to explain, and God knows, Ted wasn't going to make any apologies or excuses. Those of us who knew him appreciated that Ted was not a drinker and in his career had never been seen in a drunken state.

With a grin, Ted conceded that he had been tricked into making this particular trip to San Diego because he thought he had come to honor his old friend Breitbard. After a few more remarks, mostly to praise others, Ted thanked San Diego, Breitbard, and the audience another time and then, as if embarrassed by any more applause, was aided by John-Henry off the stage and rushed to a waiting car. All I could say was, "Thank you, Ted. Thank you for letting so many of us say, 'I love you.'"

Yet Ted was not the only ballplayer consistently honored at events during this time period. In their retirement years, Ted and Joe DiMaggio crossed paths from time to time, as they had at the 1994 event in Citrus Hills. They were, with Stan Musial, the three best players of their generation. They would be honored at the same baseball dinners and other events where they were treated like demigods from an earlier age. Often, Ted could be bombastic, pelting people with questions and advice about hitting; often, too, Joe was a man of few words who tolerated the attention until it was time to leave without being too abrupt. On these occasions (and others), Ted spoke highly of Joe. Even if there was no affection between them (other than by extension for Dominic's brother), Ted always showed a high degree of respect for Joe.

"It made me mad as hell that Ted would say Joe was 'the best ballplayer of my generation,' and one night at a restaurant I shouted, 'Bullshit!' and marched off into the bathroom," recalled Bobby Knight. "People at the adjoining table said that while I was gone, "Ted told them I was 'the smartest goddamn guy' he'd ever met."

Ted took it hard in late 1998 when he heard that Joe, soon to turn 82, was very sick. He began to call Dominic daily for updates on his brother's condition, which eventually included that Joe's cancer had spread and he was terminally ill. Ted genuinely cared—and not just for Joe, but understanding the impact his death would have on Dominic.

Sadly for him, Ted's most difficult relationships were with his wives—all three of them—and his three children. The wonderful biographies by Leigh Montville and Ben Bradlee Jr. provide plenty of details, so no need for me to weigh in. Ironically, Ted's longest and apparently most satisfying relationship was with the woman he did *not* marry. After his third divorce, Ted reconnected with Louise Kaufman, a longtime family friend whom he affectionately (most of the time) called "Lou." They were together as a couple for 20 years. When she died in August 1993, Ted was devastated. Some solace was that many people whom he had befriended and helped over the years in turn reached out to comfort him.

In the years that followed, Ted's powerful body finally began to be weakened by the aging process. Later in the 1990s, he suffered two strokes. His strong physical constitution and spirit were what most likely allowed him to survive them at all and the rehabilitation work that came afterward. Still, as Ted approached 80, he grew weaker. The discovery of a leaky heart valve and the medical determination that he would probably not survive the operation to fix it made his situation more precarious.

By the All-Star Game in 1999, Ted was mostly confined to a wheelchair. The game that July was held at Fenway Park. Not only was it the 60th anniversary of Ted's rookie season with the Red Sox, the All-Century Team would be introduced to the Boston crowd and the millions watching on television. To no one's surprise, Ted had been selected, joining the other immortals who belong on the Mt. Olympus of Major League Baseball.

Another member of the team who couldn't wait to be with Ted at the game was Tony Gwynn. In the history of the National League, only Tony and Honus Wagner won eight batting titles. The ever-loyal Gwynn spent his entire career, 20 seasons, with the Padres. His Hall of Fame résumé includes a lifetime .338 average with 3,141 hits. In over 10,000 plate appearances, he struck out only 434 times. There was a natural attraction between Tony and Ted, both left-handed hitters who dominated in their time, yet Ted didn't meet Tony on a regular basis until the 1990s, and that was whenever Ted would return home to San Diego.

Tony Gwynn Jr. recalls: "Ted thought my dad was much taller [Gwynn was a half foot shorter than Ted's 6-3] and was surprised that he was stockier. His first reaction was, 'Why don't you drive the ball more?' My dad loved to hit the ball the opposite way, wearing out the hole between third and short. He complained to Ted that it was getting tougher and tougher. Pitchers were throwing more and more inside, making it difficult to go inside-out with his swing. Ted advised, 'When they come inside, let them have it, pull those pitches with power.' He said to my dad, 'You're capable of hitting 25 to 30 home runs.'"

The light went on for Gwynn in 1997. He finished with a career-high 17 home runs, while producing a .372 average. He collected 49 doubles and drove in 119, striking out only 28 times. Not only did Gwynn have his most productive season, pitchers started staying away from pitching him inside, *exactly* what Tony wanted them to do ... out over the plate, right into his natural swing to all fields, especially the path through the third-to-short hole.

In 1999, Tony was injured and wasn't planning on attending the All-Star game in Boston until the commissioner's office called to tell him Ted had requested Gwynn be there. Fans will long remember the pregame ceremonies, a powerful emotional scene when Ted Williams was driven into the stadium from center field accompanied by the supporting large cast of All-Stars . . . even tipping his cap. Gwynn was there to support a wobbly Ted Williams when he stood to toss out the first pitch. Because of the strokes he didn't see well, and Tony gave guidance, pointing him toward home plate. Tony considered it a big thrill, and an immense honor, that Ted would select him. (Incidentally, Ted gave the All-Star jacket that he wore that night to longtime pal Bob Breitbard for display at the San Diego Hall of Champions Museum in Balboa Park.)

I had the privilege of broadcasting San Diego Padres games with the great Tony Gwynn, until his premature death in 2014. We certainly shared Ted Williams as a hero. Tony's longtime agent, John Boggs—who was the visitors' batboy at RFK Stadium in Washington in 1969 when Ted was first-year manager of the Senators—recalled for me the time when Ted and Tony first met:

"I'd never seen Tony more enthused than after his first ever luncheon with Ted after they met at Ted's Hitter's Museum in 1994. We flew home to San Diego from Florida, and Tony was bubbling over with excitement. All he could talk about was Ted. During their animated [wasn't Ted always?] conversation, Ted, as per usual, quizzed Tony in his ever-commanding voice, and Tony, although nervous, was passing the test. After all, Gwynn grew up studying Ted's *Science of Hitting* and clearly was well schooled in the Williams hitting theory. Ted would ask what Tony was looking for on any given count and Tony would answer. Ted would bellow, 'C-o-r-r-e-c-t!' Another major hit for Mr. Padre. As Ted would repeat over again, 'History is made on the inner third of the plate,' all of which was to encourage Tony to pull those pitches with power. One of the questions Williams would ask good hitters was do you smell wood burning when you make contact. Most didn't know what he was talking about. Gwynn did. He smelled the burning effect created by the friction of bat vs. ball on a foul tip. Ted once picked up Tony's bat and faked picking his teeth with it. Indeed, it was small, gave Tony more control. Tony always referred to the Thumper as Mr. Williams, explaining that he was talking to 'The Master.'"

Back to the '99 All-Star Game: First, the other members of the All-Century Team were introduced. Then it was Ted's turn. He entered from center field in a golf cart driven by Al Forester, a former member of the Fenway Park grounds crew beginning in 1957. It was a grand entrance indeed as the Boston fans cheered the man who was now indisputably the greatest living ball player. The cart passed by the right-field bullpens, turned right at the Pesky Pole, cruised slowly past the Red Sox dugout, then behind home plate and past the visitors' dugout. Adding to the adulation was the applause of the All-Century Team and the present-day American and National League All-Stars, who understood that this was a moment in baseball history never to be repeated. Ted kept waving his white hat (a Hitter.com hat John-Henry had rather crassly persuaded him to wear) enthusiastically, thanking the Boston crowd, the love on both sides finally shared and embraced.

Forester turned right at third base and brought Ted to the pitcher's mound, where he was surrounded by adoring players. Just touching Ted was like a religious experience. They wouldn't leave him despite the pleas from the public address announcer. At last, Gwynn was able to help him out of the cart, to throw the first pitch, to former Red Sox catcher Carlton Fisk.

Ted went home to Florida, not sure how much time he had left, but buoyed by the universal love he had received in Boston. And he decided not to go down without a fight. In January 2001, he did survive surgery—all 10 hours of it—to fix the heart valve. But it soon became clear that the operation had only bought a fairly short amount of time.

During one of Ted's hospital stays in his last year, former Yankees rivals Bobby Brown and Jerry Coleman made the pilgrimage to pay Ted a visit. They were escorted to his room and found Ted lying with his back turned away from the door. Hearing the visitors enter, Ted rolled to his side, saw Coleman, and said, "Fuckin' hit." And that was it. He rolled back and faced the wall. More than six decades had passed, and, both having seen combat in Korea, Ted had yet to forget or forgive that freak Coleman hit that drove in three runs to win the pennant for New York in the last game of the 1949 season.

The Teammates does such a wonderful job of describing Ted's last months and especially the trip to Florida that Dominic DiMaggio, Johnny Pesky, and Dick Flavin made by car to visit him in October 2001 that there is no sense repeating it here. (Bobby Doerr's wife had also been debilitated by strokes, and caring for her at their home in Oregon meant he could not join his friends in Florida.) Suffice to say that the visit cheered him up immensely, especially the songs the visitors sang and Flavin reciting his composition TEDDY AT THE BAT. With Dick's permission, I am including it here:

TEDDY AT THE BAT
(With apologies to Ernest Lawrence Thayer)

The outlook wasn't brilliant for the Red Sox nine that day,
The score stood four to two with but one inning left to play.
So when Stephens died at first and Tebbetts did the same
A pallor wreathed the features of the patrons of the game.

A straggling few got up to go, leaving there the rest
With the hope that springs eternal within the human breast.
They thought if only Teddy could get a whack at that—
They'd put even money now with Teddy at the bat.

But Dom preceded Teddy and Pesky was on deck.
The first of them was in a slump. The other was a wreck.

But Dom let drive a single, to the wonderment of all,
And Pesky, of all people, tore the cover off the ball.
When the dust had lifted, and they saw what had occurred,
There was Johnny safe on second and Dominic on third.

Then from that gladdened multitude went up a joyous yell,
It rumbled in the mountains and rattled in the dell.
It struck upon the hillside and rebounded on the flat,
For Teddy, Teddy Ballgame, was advancing to the bat.

There was ease in Teddy's manner as he stepped into his place,
There was pride in Teddy's bearing and a smile on Teddy's face.
And when, responding to the cheers he lightly doffed his hat,
(I'm making that part up)
No stranger in the crowd could doubt 'twas Teddy at the bat.

Ten thousand eyes were on him as he wiped his hands with dirt,
Five thousand tongues applauded as he wiped them on his shirt.
Then when the writhing pitcher ground the ball into his hip,
Defiance gleamed in Teddy's eyes, a sneer curled Teddy's lip.

And now the leather covered sphere came hurtling through the air,
And Teddy stood a-watching it in haughty grandeur there.
Close by the sturdy batsman the ball unheeded sped.
"That ain't my style," said Teddy. "Strike one!" the umpire said.

From the benches black with people went up a muffled roar,
Like the beating of the storm waves on the stern and distant shore.
"Kill him! Kill the umpire!" someone shouted on the stand,
And it's likely they'd have killed him had not Teddy raised his hand.

With a smile of Christian charity great Teddy's visage shown.
He stilled the rising tumult and bade the game go on.
He signaled the pitcher, and once more the spheroid flew.
But Teddy still ignored it, and the umpire said, "Strike two!"

"Fraud!" cried the maddened thousands, and the echo answered fraud.
But one scornful look from Teddy and the audience was awed.
They saw his face grow stern and cold, they saw his muscles strain,
And they knew that Teddy wouldn't let that ball go by again.

The sneer is gone from Teddy's lip; his teeth are clenched in hate.
He pounds with cruel vengeance his bat upon the plate.
And now the pitcher holds the ball, and now he lets it go,
And now the air is shattered by the force of Teddy's blow.

Oh, somewhere in this land of ours the sun is shining bright,
The band is playing somewhere, and somewhere hearts are light,
And somewhere men are laughing, and somewhere children shout.
And they're going wild at Fenway Park 'cause Teddy hit one out!

Ted's home in Hernando was a good four-hour drive from Palm Beach, a haul for a man in his 80s with a cranky back; but still, during Ted's last year, Dominic visited as often as he could manage. The two elderly outfielders reminisced about their own "core four" on the Red Sox, other teammates, and the close calls of the 1946-50 years. Sometimes, Ted fell into a depression, feeling betrayed by his once-magnificent physique and knowing his poor health was irreversible. Dominic was relentlessly calm and supportive. When Dominic wasn't there, because he was at home in the Palm Beach area or up in Massachusetts, he called Ted every day. "Yes, I'm here, Dommie, I'm here," Ted would reassure him.

During those last few months, there were fewer times that Ted could reassure his old friend that he was still there. When the 2002 baseball season began, Dominic called every day not only to check on Ted, but to give him the scores, beginning, of course, with the Red Sox. (It would not be until two years later that Boston won its first world championship since 1918, the year Ted was born.) Some days, Ted would lose consciousness during the conversation, and his attendant would hang up the phone.

This happened during the call from Dominic on July 4. Dominic told the attendant, "Please tell Ted I called." When he called the next day, he learned the news: Ted Williams, age 83, died in an Inverness, Florida, hospital on July 5, 2002.

I've often felt death is surreal, so hard to comprehend. Birth is magical. Suddenly, a new life is here. But death? How could a man of such animation be silent . . . no longer here? Learning of Ted's death, I closed my eyes, hoping to hear the noise of immortality.

That month, I and several other friends of Ted's held a memorial service for him in San Diego. In my remarks, I recounted a story from his youth that Ted had shared with me. One winter day, during a rare San Diego rainstorm, Ted and his brother Danny devised an indoor game of hitting a hard-shelled black walnut with a broomstick. Ted said his brother hit one back at him, striking him directly in the right eye. "Never did see well again out of that eye," he said.

"Oh my!" I thought. Here's a man once measured in the military with 20-10 vision, a man who could count the stitches on a fastball, complaining that his sight was impaired by a childhood accident. If not for a misguided walnut, Ted might have hit .500!

Three months later, the Anaheim Angels of Gene Autry in their 42nd season would win the World Series for the first (and so far only) time. Though invited, I was unable to attend the final game at Anaheim Stadium, as they defeated the San Francisco Giants in Game Seven. In fact, I didn't even see the game on television. I was in Kansas City working the Sunday telecast of an NFL game for CBS. The night before, while prepping for my football play-by-play, I yelled and screamed like an obnoxious, annoying fan in my hotel room, as the Angels pulled out a remarkable 6-5 comeback win. Now, it was Sunday, and my schedule dictated my working the football telecast, racing to the KC airport, and flying back to San Diego, occasionally getting a partial World Series score.

In midair halfway through the flight, the pilot clicked the interrupt to announce, "For those of you that may be interested, the Angels have won the World Series." And the Enberg emotional dam burst again. Seeing me shaking and sobbing, the woman seated next to me, not knowing my personal involvement, pulled out her Rosary and started praying. She thought something very bad was about to happen to the plane. I assured her that everything, *everything*, was just fine, in fact, heavenly. My joy was for all those who had loyally followed the Angels. It was for all the Angels' games, win or lose, good or bad, that I had broadcast, but most of all, it was for the biggest Angel of all, Mr. Autry, who sadly didn't live long enough to embrace this glorious climactic moment. (The Singing Cowboy died four years earlier at age 91, ironically during the 1998 World Series.) And I was finally letting lose about losing Ted, as a friend and a baseball idol. Gosh, I would've loved to call him when I got home to talk about the Angels' victory . . . and to hear him explain with complete authority how it was accomplished.

I eventually wiped away the tears, leaned back in my seat, and silently smiled and smiled all the rest of the way home. Oh my, the halo shined that night!

To this day, I still wonder at my good fortune. Ted Williams was an influence long before I met him. I dreamed about being Ted Williams. I taught myself to bat left-handed to copy him. I was in the stands to cheer his awesome swing. Then, to get to know him and have him share much of himself and his philosophy with me completed such a beautiful cycle. My dreams have taken me to a great place. Too bad every kid's idol can't become his friend.

Did Ted really consider me a friend? Maybe it's presumptuous of me to say that. It doesn't matter. He included me in many fascinating conversations, and he seemed to genuinely appreciate my work. "Damn it, Enberg," he proclaimed once, "you're the best there is."

That's good enough.

This year, the centennial of Ted Williams, will also see the 30th birthday of the first son Barbara and I welcomed into this world. His name is Ted Enberg.

EPILOGUE

In July 2016, in my final year as a broadcaster of San Diego Padres games, that city's *Union-Tribune* newspaper published this essay of mine. I think it sums up my feelings about my favorite sport. It's my love letter to our national pastime.

Why do I love thee . . . let me count the ways.

The game teases and caresses all my senses.

The promise of sweet sounds of bat against ball and within its echo a glove swallowing hope.

The subtle scent of the infield's morning mow.

The olfactory bombardment of an old ballpark's stale beer.

The baseball barking of umpires and concessionaires.

The chatter of spikes on the concrete steps.

The classic Shakespearean confrontation of best hitter versus best pitcher.

Sunshine and shadows; day to night.

Spring hopes to autumn reality.

The distinct beauty of the baseball field's geometry . . . squares, circles, rectangles, a pentagon, and lines to infinity.

The sight of a ball's towering Ruthian flight to a distant landing, pushed to its destination by a crescendo of awe.

Getting dirty so cleanly in the graceful completion of a fall-away hook slide.

The perfect interception of a laser liner by a radar correct outfielder . . . and sometimes the daring dive to accomplish the mission.

To marvel at Gwynn's mastery of an inside out missile, deftly directed through the 5.5 target.

To comprehend the sleight of hand of Brooks Robinson, magically reducing doubles into 5-3s.

To acknowledge the subtle arrogance of a Carew drag bunt.

Jackie's audacious dash to a theft of home.

To share with an audience the extraordinary late innings' drama of a pitcher's relentless omnipotence, grunting and grinding to a hitless game. In my privileged 60 years, the no-hitter is the single most exciting experience ever as a sportscaster. What blessed theater! (See Nolan Ryan.)

Ted Williams. How splendid the San Diego Splinter.

The anthem reverently sung by a children's choir.

The communal crooning every 7th inning to root, root, root for the home team.

The universal smile of joy of any fan of any age when securing a precious foul ball.

And, oh my, the immaculately executed ballet of a double play.

As the lyric goes, these are just a few of my favorite things.

And we all know its poetry doesn't end there. Baseball never ends . . . there. That's why we embrace it, share it, score it, play it—a generational game connecting us inexorably with a grandfather's past and the unknowns of Little League hope.

I've taken great privilege and joy in reporting the unique beauty of our game—each game providing its strengths, subtleties, spirit, and sober disappointments. I finally have come to understand that baseball is a religion. Hey, I've worked for the Angels and Padres, and Lord knows during the course of a season we all pray a lot.

Amen.